NAVIES IN VIOLENT PEACE

Also by James Cable
GUNBOAT DIPLOMACY
THE ROYAL NAVY AND THE SIEGE OF BILBAO
*GUNBOAT DIPLOMACY, 1919–1979 (Second Edition)
*BRITAIN'S NAVAL FUTURE
*DIPLOMACY AT SEA
*THE GENEVA CONFERENCE OF 1954 ON INDOCHINA
*POLITICAL INSTITUTIONS AND ISSUES IN BRITAIN

As Grant Hugo
BRITAIN IN TOMORROW'S WORLD
APPEARANCE AND REALITY IN INTERNATIONAL RELATIONS

* Also published by Macmillan

Navies in Violent Peace

James Cable

MACMILLAN

First published 1989

Published by
THE MACMILLAN PRESS LTD
Houndmills, Basingstoke, Hampshire RG21 2XS
and London
Companies and representatives
throughout the world

Typeset by Wessex Typesetters
(Division of The Eastern Press Ltd)
Frome, Somerset

Printed in the People's Republic of China

British Library Cataloguing in Publication Data
Cable, James. 1920–
Navies in violent peace
1. Sea-power.
I. Title.
359
ISBN 0–333–45929–6

For Viveca, as always

Contents

Introduction   ix

1   Total War at Sea   1

2   Limited War at Sea   16

3   Proxy War at Sea   32

4   The Persistence of Gunboat Diplomacy   39

5   Gunboat Diplomacy in the 1980s and Beyond   57

6   Showing the Flag   71

7   Estate Management at Sea   82

8   Piracy and Terrorism at Sea   92

9   Who Needs Ocean-going Navies?   102

10 Arms Control at Sea   112

Notes and References   129

Select Bibliography   140

Index   142

Introduction

[We] must recognize the chief characteristics of the modern era –
a permanent state of what I call violent peace . . . the continuing
and widespread existence of localized conflicts and crises. . . . In
this age of violent peace, the Navy is on the front lines already,
and will be for the foreseeable future. – ADMIRAL JAMES D. WATKINS,
USN[1]

Today's Naval Commander must have the qualities of an experienced politician. . . . – M. S. GORBACHEV[2]

We live in a time of change. People have believed as much in most
eras of the human race, but today there is more evidence to back
the notion. If we assume that *homo sapiens* first appeared about
35 000 BC, then the population of the world took nearly 37 000 years
to reach the first billion by 1850 AD. The second came only 75 years
later, in 1925. Now we are approaching 5 billion and by the year
2000 we shall probably be over 6 billion. No doubt growth will then
diminish, as it did in the United Kingdom, which tripled its population
during the nineteenth century, but will come nowhere near doubling
it in the twentieth. Even so, more growth is a disturbing prospect
and one calculated to increase the likely incidence of human conflict.

Curiously enough this has not so far matched the mounting
demographic curve. A recent and systematic study of war between
1816 and 1980 concluded:

[There] were 67 interstate wars and 51 imperial and colonial wars,
leading directly to the death of almost 31 million military personnel. . . . Looking at the entire period there is no evidence that
international war has been on the increase. The number of
wars, the battle deaths, and the nation months have fluctuated
considerably over time, with the 'average' decade seeing 7.9 wars,
over 400 nation months of war, and over 2 million battle deaths.
Nor have later wars generally been any more intense in terms of
death per capita or per nation month.

The authors reached rather similar conclusions about the 106 major
civil wars during their period.[3]

These calculations could scarcely be expected to apply if the world were ever faced with the kind of total war that nuclear weapons have now made possible. It is probably fear of this horrendous unknown that has so far induced the major powers, for over 40 years, to restrict themselves to limited war. The Germans, Italians and Japanese have avoided even that, but the torch they dropped has been seized by other nations, who bore the brunt of the fighting in Korea, Indochina, the Middle East and the Persian Gulf.

Forty years is too brief a period to permit firm conclusions, but the fear of a total war that might prove final is not the only trend that seems to be emerging. Europe has been unusually free from war, Greece and Cyprus providing the main exceptions. Yet neither the greater prevalence of conflict beyond the seas, nor the proliferation of nation-states (five times as many as in 1816), nor the sheer number of navies have led to any increased incidence of war at sea. On the contrary, there has only been one genuinely naval war since 1945.

So what are the world's 105 navies going to do in an era of violent peace? That it is violent the media remind us every day. That it is peace is a matter of opinion and largely depends on where you live. That it might soon get much better seems unlikely – almost as unlikely as the notion that anyone could win a total war.

Limited war and proxy war may only occasionally need warships, but they are contingencies against which some countries will continue to want a measure of naval cover. Warships provided for such purposes may more often be employed in gunboat diplomacy, in showing the flag, in estate management and in coping with pirates and terrorists. These are important tasks and the last has received too little attention in recent years. Nevertheless sailors in many countries can expect increasing competition for scarce resources from soldiers and airmen sceptical of the value of ocean-going navies. These are also targets for the advocates of various forms of arms control.

That is the scope of the book: political requirements for, and political constraints on, the employment of naval force.

This is both a bad and a good moment – approaching the century's last decade – to take a forward look. It is bad because, in the words of a leading article in *The Times*,

> A modern navy is a totally untried weapon of warfare. It is the resultant of a host of more or less conflicting theories of attack and defence.[4]

That was written in 1889, but it remains largely true today, certainly of the US and Soviet navies. The Falklands War of 1982, for instance, did not provide enough relevant evidence for an informed judgement of the validity of the American Maritime Strategy.

One reason for thinking it a good moment is of an entirely superstitious character. When previous centuries have reached their later eighties, omens have appeared. One scarcely needs to mention the Armada in 1588; or Dartmouth, admiral of King James II in 1688, letting the Dutch fleet slip through the Straits to bear William of Orange to victory and Glorious Revolution. And everyone knows that the French Revolution of 1789 led to the longest of major naval wars, which killed more British sailors than the Great War of 1914–18.[5]

Last century, however, the symbols were more subtle. In 1886 Captain John Fisher was appointed Britain's Director of Naval Ordnance. In 1887 Crown Prince Wilhelm of Germany (he became Kaiser the following year) chose Captain Alfred von Tirpitz to accompany him to Queen Victoria's Golden Jubilee, where there were still ships with sails at the Naval Review.[6] The scene-shifters (Fisher and Tirpitz each transformed the navies they eventually headed) had arrived to set the stage for the First World War. And, in 1889, there came the first whisper of the Second: the birth on 20 April of Adolf Hitler.

In purely naval terms, of course, this was a more changeable era than our own. In 1982 HMS HERMES was 23 years old when she became Admiral Woodward's flagship in the Falklands War. In 1987 half the carriers in the US Navy were even older: two of them (MIDWAY and CORAL SEA) had served more than the 40 years accumulated by HMS VICTORY before the battle of Trafalgar in 1805. The four battleships still employed by the US Navy dated from the Second World War.

A hundred years ago, however, 'the British Admiralty were opposed to great battleship programmes because of the rapid evolution of the art of naval construction, which made a large increase of vessels liable to become obsolete in a short space of time'.[7] Admiral Hewett dismissed the Jubilee Naval Review of 1887 with the caustic comment: 'most of what you see is mere ullage'.[8] No British battleship then afloat survived to fight in any naval war.

Politics were even more volatile. No navy in the years that ended the nineteenth century and began the twentieth could maintain the durable assumptions of our own era, in which the national composition of Red and Blue Fleets has scarcely altered for four decades. On either side some countries were less firmly committed than others, but only one important navy seems to have switched wartime targets and that is the navy of the still inscrutable Chinese. In the quarter century after 1889, on the other hand, most major navies were periodically required to recast their ideas, sometimes accepting as allies the very navies previously typecast as enemies.

Stability today is only relative. The central balance trembles a little at each external shock from the post-imperial turmoil that troubles so much of the Third World. Even the black picture often painted of the current of events sweeping the human canoe towards Niagara cannot be entirely dismissed. It merely seems less likely than it did a quarter of a century ago. The armed truce of the Super Powers has now survived such repeated and many-sided provocations that it might last some years longer.

At any rate it is worth assuming that future conflict will be neither general, nor total, nor final. It facilitates discussion of the likely functions of navies. Nor is violent peace just the comfortable prognosis of those who shrink from the idea of total war. Caspar Weinberger himself endorsed the view that 'low-intensity conflict will remain the most likely and the most enduring threat to our security'.[9]

JAMES CABLE

1 Total War at Sea

> The sides, having discussed key security issues, and conscious of
> the special responsibility of the USSR and the US for maintaining
> peace, have agreed that a nuclear war cannot be won and must
> never be fought – GORBACHEV–REAGAN, 1985[1]

In the last quarter of the twentieth century total war means nuclear
war. This is a difficult subject to address. The literature devoted to it
is naturally copious. Every aspect of the problem has been tackled
and from most points of view. Henry Kissinger's impressive record
as a major actor in international politics adds to the significance of
the book that launched his career in 1957: *Nuclear Weapons and
Foreign Policy*. He has had few rivals, but many successors and
imitators. Scientists have always had much to contribute to the
debate. In 1950 Einstein warned his American television audience of
the risk of 'general annihilation'. In 1983 a conference of scientists
at Cambridge, Massachusets was told that war might well be followed
by an almost equally catastrophic 'nuclear winter'. Crudely summar-
ised, the theory was that enough nuclear explosions would produce
smoke and dust in sufficient quantities to obscure the light of the
sun, sharply lower the temperature and, when combined with other
effects, jeopardise the survival of the species in at least the northern
hemisphere.[2]

This was an idea which only the occurrence of nuclear war
could conclusively prove or disprove, but it was taken seriously by
organisations as little disposed to alarmist pacifism as the United
States Department of Defense and the International Institute for
Strategic Studies.[3] Other aspects of nuclear war have received no less
attention from academics in a variety of disciplines, from political
and strategic analysts, from ecclesiastics, journalists and politicians.

Much of the information at their disposal has come from
governments. More has been revealed in the United States than
anywhere else, but the flow of comment from military sources in the
Soviet Union began after the death of Stalin and has gradually
increased. Until 1980 British governments were more reticent, as the
Chinese still remain. The French attitude to disclosure has been
erratic, but unofficial authors have long managed to acquire knowledge and to express views in Britain and France alike. Nor is it only

1

in those states that actually deploy nuclear weapons that there is a lively debate concerning the possible occurrence and the probable nature of nuclear war. In many countries and in most walks of life there are people anxious to utter an opinion on a subject of some importance to the human race.

This must include the writers of fiction. In 1914 H. G. Wells was guessing (even Rutherford did not take the first step before 1919), but by 1932 Harold Nicolson had some grounds for using the explosion of an atomic bomb as the dénouement of his novel *Public Faces*. He was nevertheless years ahead of any government or most scientists. Even today voters in democratic countries probably derive their notions of the nature of nuclear war quite as much from novelists or the fantasies of cinema and television as they do from more earnest efforts to enlighten them. This is not surprising. Imagination – the main quality required in the pundits of nuclear war – comes more easily to writers of fiction.

There has not, after all, ever been a nuclear war, one in which both sides used such weapons. In August 1945 an American atomic bomb of what would now be considered relatively low yield (under 20 kilotons) exploded over Hiroshima and another over Nagasaki. Estimates of the numbers killed in each city vary greatly either side of 100 000, but the casualties were of the same order of magnitude as those inflicted earlier that year by the British conventional attack on Dresden or the American on Tokyo. The difference was that one bomb had produced a devastation previously requiring half a million incendiaries and hundreds of aircraft.

A week later, the Japanese Government, who had no prior knowledge that nuclear weapons existed or would be used against their country, accepted the demand for surrender first made to them on 26 July. Whether the bombs had to be dropped to elicit this Japanese decision has since been much debated. There is something to be said for Churchill's view:

> it would be a mistake to suppose that the fate of Japan was settled by the atomic bomb. Her defeat was certain before the first bomb fell, and was brought about by overwhelming maritime power.[4]

The dropping, on two August days over 40 years ago, of two small bombs is the only instance so far of the use of nuclear weapons in actual hostilities. Since that date many much more powerful weapons have been developed and tested. Governments have been given by their military and scientific advisers elaborate predictions of how these weapons might be employed and with what results. Strategies have been devised for many different kinds of nuclear war. Never before has so much human intelligence been devoted to the analysis of hypothetical future conflict. And these toiling brains have been reinforced by an array of computers that did not even exist in 1939, let alone in 1914. The analytical resources at the disposal of strategic foresight are unprecedented. It is the relevant experience that is a trifle scanty.

In 1916, for instance, the British and German fleets that met at Jutland were much larger and more powerful than those of Russia and Japan at Tsushima in 1905 or than the British and German forces in such minor naval encounters as Coronel, the Falklands or the Dogger Bank. But neither the ships, nor their armament, nor the tactics employed were radically different. Nor were they in 1941, when all the British battleships that fought at Matapan (BARHAM, VALIANT and WARSPITE) had also been at Jutland. In 1987, however, the International Institute for Strategic Studies estimated that the United States had 13 873 *strategic* nuclear warheads and the Soviet Union 11 044.[5] None of these had a destructive power less than 40 kilotons and many achieved a megaton or more. When tactical weapons, those of intermediate range and those belonging to lesser powers are added in, there may exist nearly 50 000 warheads, with an aggregate yield approaching 15 000 megatons. This is not the same world, not even a comparable world, as that of August 1945, when there existed two nuclear warheads with an aggregate yield of under 40 kilotons.

So everything that is now said or written about nuclear war, by governments or by agitators, by generals or by journalists, by scientists or by priests, is guesswork. They do not know, because nobody has experienced nuclear war. Even the unfortunate Japanese victims of those minor incidents in 1945 did not understand what was happening to them.

The arguments may be hypothetical, but the debate about nuclear war is real. It will not come to an end, nor will the military planning that accompanies it, just because Gorbachev and Reagan agreed in 1985 'that a nuclear war cannot be won and must never be fought'.[6] The two leaders hurried home from Geneva to add another 5000 strategic warheads – over the next two years – to their already substantial nuclear armouries.

Words are not much of an antidote to nuclear weapons. Little happened when Nixon and Brezhnev agreed on 26 May 1972 'that nuclear war would have devastating consequences for all mankind'.[7] In February 1977, for instance, the US Joint Chiefs-of-Staff defined 'US strategic nuclear strategy . . . as maintaining military strength sufficient to deter attack but also, in the event deterrence fails, sufficient to provide a war-fighting capability to escalation and terminate the war on terms acceptable to the United States'.[8] A year later Marshal Ogarkov declared:

> Soviet military strategy proceeds from the view that if the Soviet Union is thrust into a nuclear war the Soviet people and their Armed Forces need to be prepared for the most severe and protracted trial.[9]

His reference to 'the objective possibility of achieving victory' was properly cautious.

This contrast between political leaders prophesying doom and military leaders preparing for it is not new. In December 1953 President Eisenhower told the United Nations that a nuclear war could destroy civilisation and was echoed, three months later, by Malenkov, then Soviet Prime Minister: 'the destruction of world civilisation'.[10] On 20 May 1954 the US Joint Chiefs-of-Staff, planning to support the crumbling French military position in Indochina, recorded: 'atomic weapons will be used whenever it is to our military advantage'.[11]

DETERRENCE

Neither long immunity nor the recent enthusiasm for token nuclear disarmament of Reagan and Gorbachev should persuade anyone that nuclear war has become impossible. Victory may be improbable and survival uncertain, but plans are still being made to fight nuclear war. In Western countries such preparations are rationalised as deterrence. For Britain and France that is plausible. Each has strategic sub-marines, of which one or more would probably survive a Russian attack on either country and be able at least to destroy Moscow, even if the United States did nothing. On the other hand, Britain and France could neither defeat the Soviet Union in nuclear war, nor significantly increase the ability of the United States to do so, nor themselves expect to escape extinction as nation-states.

It is worth remarking that, for Britain and France, such deterrence is at present necessarily naval. France has aircraft capable (if refuelled en route) of carrying nuclear weapons to the Soviet Union, but not so many that the Soviet Union could not hope, in a surprise attack, to destroy them on their airfields, or to sink the two aircraft carriers or to intercept the aircraft that escaped before they crossed the borders of Russia. French land-based missiles are even more vulnerable. The Soviet Union would have much less chance of detecting a submerged submarine in time to destroy it before missiles could be launched.

Even the Super Powers, each with over a thousand land-based missiles deployed in hardened silos, have felt the need to reinforce what the enemy would preceive as their ability to retaliate after a surprise attack. The United States has supplemented its land-based missiles with long-range bombers, some of which should already be airborne when the enemy missiles arrived. The Soviet Union is expanding and modernising its long-range bomber force, but already deploys even more strategic submarines than the United States, though American submarines could launch twice as many warheads. In spite of efforts by both sides to improve submarine detection – a contest in which geography as well as expertise favours the United States – enough submarines (particularly those able to remain in home waters, thanks to the long range of their missiles) are likely to survive even a surprise attack to permit retaliation on a scale that ought to deter a first strike.

It is the superior survivability of the submarine that gives it such prominence in the deterrent strategy of all the nuclear powers except China (which has yet to deploy submarine-launched ballistic missiles of truly strategic range). Naturally other warships, particularly strike carriers, have a contribution to make, but they are more vulnerable both to surprise attack and to attrition. The relevance of attrition is that deterrence is no longer a single-shot concept. In the days of American nuclear dominance and the doctrine of 'massive retaliation', it was supposed that a solitary trip-wire – a Soviet invasion of West Germany, for instance – might be enough to unleash a full nuclear bombardment. Since the attainment of approximate nuclear parity between the Super Powers, more gradual approaches to total war are usually envisaged. Nuclear weapons might initially be employed only in the theatre of operations, or at sea, or outside the metropolitan territory of either Super Power. In the eyes of Americans and Russians nuclear war would be 'limited', because their own soil would be immune and their central strategic system would not be fully committed.

This is the theory. Could two enemies actually contain their conflict and endure casualties on even a limited nuclear scale long enough for fighting to end in negotiation rather than lead to escalation? Some people seem to think so:

> the best way to halt a Pact offensive on the Central Front . . . is a very early and very large theater nuclear strike by NATO . . . the Pact offensive would die before it could really begin.[12]

An even more alarming view (because it came from an United States Secretary of Defense) was expressed by James Schlesinger:

> once three or four or five nuclear weapons are employed, sensible political leaders would look around aghast at the consequences – and say 'Let's stop right here!'[13]

Perhaps they would. Perhaps the Russians are only bluffing when they talk of the inevitability of escalation. But it is also possible to regard any use of nuclear weapons as shifting conflict into a new gear. Most people understand the need to limit political or military action in order to avoid any employment of nuclear weapons. Once the first nuclear explosion has occurred, it will be more difficult to agree on the precise stage at which retaliation should be renounced, objectives abandoned, concessions made, for fear of worse. Between conventional and nuclear conflict there may be much the same jagged break as between peace and war. It is uncertain whether any later change will be politically so obvious. Escalation could go faster than debate and negotiation. Those waiting submarines, the ultimate sanction, might receive their orders earlier than the theorists of nuclear strategy suppose.

Before that happened, of course, nuclear weapons of other kinds might well be discharged from different warships. Cruise missiles, for instance, could be launched against targets in the land theatre of operations from ships at sea. The relative emphasis accorded to deterrence and war-fighting in the strategic doctrines of the two Super Powers has received much attention from Western scholars. Although opinions differ considerably, the consensus seems to be that, in the Russian view, the enemy cannot be deterred by the mere danger of nuclear war, but only by the fear that, for him, victory would be impossible. There is quite as much emphasis in Russian writing as there is in American on the tendency to aggression inherent in the rival political system and on the consequent risk of suffering a surprise attack. According to Admiral Chernavin, 'surprise was and still is the principal method the imperialist aggressors use to start combat operations'.[14]

In the Soviet Union, as in Western countries, the orthodox view is that nuclear war would be (as Boris Ponomarev put it in 1983) 'catastrophic for all civilisation',[15] but it is still being planned and, in East and West alike, there are people who think it could be won, and occasionally say so. It would be unduly optimistic to suppose that talk of fighting a nuclear war is intended only to reinforce the credibility of deterrence.

Nor is a surprise nuclear attack the only threat against which deterrence is sought. The European members of NATO have always believed themselves vulnerable to a conventional offensive on land, whether directed against the Central Front or the northern or southern flanks. The balance of conventional forces in place favours the Warsaw Pact, whose generals might hope to overrun the defenders in a sudden assault before reinforcements could arrive in sufficient strength. Massive retaliation from the United States being no longer credible as an initial response, NATO fell back on the notion that tactical nuclear weapons or those of intermediate range might provide a substitute. It has never been obvious why the prospect of such weapons being used within the theatre of operations, where the Russians could match them, should be more alarming to the Soviet Union than to the Europeans themselves. On the other hand, a nuclear weapon exploding on Russian soil, whatever its firing-point, would naturally invite retaliation against the continental United States.

Nevertheless, in March 1986 the International Institute for Strategic Studies (IISS) confidently asserted:

> there is no reason to believe that NATO will be able to do much radically to improve its conventional defence and thus significantly to reduce its ultimate dependence on nuclear weapons.[16]

The nervous responses, in 1986 and 1987, of European leaders to American and Russian proposals for drastic reductions in the deployment of nuclear weapons of short and intermediate range rather suggest that the Institute were right. Deterring conventional attack by threatening a nuclear response may nowadays seem less convincing, but nobody in NATO has yet found a plausible alternative that is not much more expensive. No sensible Russian, of course, need worry that NATO's inferior forces might start a war by launching a conventional ground offensive.

THE MARITIME STRATEGY

The pace of naval preparation for total war has been largely set by
the United States. In the fifties they introduced bigger and faster
carriers equipped with aircraft of longer range. By 1968 that authorita-
tive Soviet strategist, Marshal Sokolovskiy, was writing:

> one of our Navy's most important tasks will be to destroy the
> enemy carrier strike forces . . . [before these could] deliver surprise
> nuclear strikes on major coastal targets . . . and possibly on targets
> much further inland.[17]

As the range of American carrier-borne aircraft grew and the
defensive screens of their parent carriers were improved, the Soviet
Navy had to be expanded, its operational perimeter extended, its
equipment upgraded and its tactics given a more aggressive edge.
When the 1973 Arab–Israeli War provoked a crisis in Super Power
relations, anti-carrier groups of the Soviet Mediterranean Squadron
(themselves equipped with tactical nuclear weapons) further raised
the temperature by simulated attacks on the carriers of the United
States Sixth Fleet.

The Soviet Navy found it more difficult to counter American
deployment during the 1960s of nuclear-powered submarines carrying
submarine-launched ballistic missiles with nuclear warheads. As the
range of these missiles was increased, the Russians tried to extend
the scope of their anti-submarine forces. It is much harder, however,
to locate and trail submarines than it is to shadow carrier task-forces.
Retaliation thus seemed more promising than defence. Yet, when
the Russians eventually deployed (it took them an entire decade)
strategic submarines of their own, these were geographically handicapped. They did not have as easy access to the ocean wastes as their
American rivals. Perhaps partly for this reason the Soviet Navy has
developed missiles of such long range that some of its strategic
submarines can remain in home waters where they are hard to find
or attack. Western writers have also suggested that the Russians may
have a 'withholding strategy' and intend to keep most of their
submarines in reserve even after the outbreak of nuclear war, so as
to be able to threaten, perhaps even to make, a final and potentially
decisive strike.

Besides these necessarily nuclear tasks (the deterrent functions of
the British and French navies were mentioned earlier) many Super
Power warships carry nuclear weapons designed for use at sea as well

as their conventional armament. As long as land war involving the Super Powers was expected to escalate rapidly and almost automatically, early resort to nuclear weapons seemed equally probable at sea: between submarines attacking convoys and the convoy escorts, for instance. Even the British navy has nuclear depth-bombs.

Easy answers have been less readily available since the establishment of nuclear parity, but there is still a tendency to regard the oceans as constituting a special case. In 1984 an American naval officer took the view that

> tactical nuclear weapons are grand ordnance against surface warships, submarines, and aircraft. The remoteness of naval conflicts and the absence of collateral damage and civilian deaths may well make war at sea a unique environment in which the nuclear firebreak is weak or nonexistent, with the link to escalation ashore very thin. Future naval conflict could become nuclear very fast.[18]

In 1986 two other American writers argued:

> Conflict at sea may be the only kind of nuclear war between superpowers that can remain localized and limited because of its remoteness from homelands and the absence of major collateral damage.[19]

These may be unduly complacent views, but it is worth considering what kind of naval war might conceivably become nuclear.

For many years the hypothesis most favoured was the Third Battle of the Atlantic: Soviet submarines trying to prevent the passage of transatlantic reinforcements for the Central Front. This scenario still has naval supporters, but others have long found it difficult to synchronise a Soviet blitzkrieg in Germany with the slower process of assembling reinforcements, loading them into ships and fighting a way for them across the ocean. A new concept has therefore emerged in recent years and is now grandly called the Maritime Strategy.

First developed in 1982, this concept was officially and publicly expounded in January 1986 by the United States Chief of Naval Operations, Admiral James D. Watkins.[20] 'Preparation for global war', the Admiral argued, 'is the critical element in ensuring deterrence'. In his view, although 'the Soviets appear to assume a future war with the West will be global in scope, violent and decisive', they would prefer to be able to concentrate on a single theatre: 'a combined-arms assault against Europe, where they would seek a quick and decisive victory'. Admiral Watkins expects most of the

Soviet Navy to remain on the defensive in home waters, but he intends to deny to the Soviet Union their preferred option of concentrating on a single theatre.

'The initial phase of the Maritime Strategy' (which Admiral Watkins calls the maritime component of the National Military Strategy) 'would be triggered by the recognition that a specific international situation has the potential to grow to a global superpower confrontation.' In this phase, before any actual fighting between Americans and Russians, the United States Navy would carry out a forward deployment – anti-submarine forces, amphibious forces, carrier battle-groups – to the Mediterranean, the Norwegian Sea, the Western Pacific. Reserves would be mobilised. Such a deployment would not only be strategically advantageous, but should have a deterrent effect.

In the next phase, once deterrence had failed and the first shot had been fired, the US Navy

> will seize the initiative as far forward as possible. Naval forces will destroy Soviet forces in the Mediterranean, Indian Ocean and other forward areas, neutralize Soviet clients and fight our way toward Soviet home waters.

Admiral Watkins lays particular emphasis on attacking Soviet submarines, including ballistic missile submarines, but he also wants to defeat Soviet air and surface forces, so that the US Navy will then be able to use their strike-power to intervene in the land battles, perhaps also to establish a beachhead for the eventual landing of armies of liberation.

In the final phase the fight would be carried to the enemy, the destruction of all Soviet fleets completed, Soviet bases threatened and the destruction of Soviet ballistic missile submarines continued until 'war termination on terms favorable to the United States and its allies'.

Not the least surprising feature of this ambitious programme is the assumption that it could be implemented without nuclear war: 'escalation solely as a result of actions at sea seems improbable, given the Soviet land orientation.' Perhaps Admiral Watkins was writing tongue-in-cheek. When he says that 'eliminating forward-deployed Soviet surface ships at the outset of the conflict . . . requires appropriate rules of engagement at the brink of war to avoid losing the battle of the first salvo', he surely has nuclear weapons in mind. When his carriers are disposed for war – other American writers have even suggested putting a battle-group into Norway's Vest Fjord to strike at the Kola bases – will they be denied the use of nuclear weapons for their own defence? What is more – for these instances could at least be accommodated by the American belief that nuclear exchanges between ships are tactical and can be confined to the sea – would the Russians allow their strategic submarines to be destroyed one by one (and it might take nuclear weapons to sink them) without even launching their missiles?

It would be presumptuous to question the Admiral's naval judgement, but there is room for doubting what, politically, he has rather taken for granted. There is, for instance, his initial premise: 'recognition that a specific international situation has the potential to grow to a global superpower confrontation'. This is not as simple as the Admiral seems to suppose.

If we consider only this century, the Japanese achieved strategic surprise against Russia at Port Arthur in 1904 and against the United States at Pearl Harbor in 1941. Earlier in that year Russia had been surprised by the German invasion and in 1973 Israel, a country whose politicians are usually as alert as the generals, was surprised by the Arabs. In 1982 General Galtieri caught the British napping in the Falklands. These were all cases in which a country long regarded as unfriendly had nevertheless not been expected to launch an attack out of the blue. The victims had counted on what NATO now calls 'political warning time': a progressive rise in the international temperature punctuated by obvious indicators of hostile intentions or military preparations.

Deliberate deception by the enemy is not the only factor which may impair the reliability of 'political warning time'. In an unpremeditated crisis there may be such general confusion that the red light is simply not recognised for what it is. On 30 June 1914, for instance, Sir Arthur Nicolson, the intelligent and knowledgeable Permanent Under-Secretary of the British Foreign Office, who had for years been warning his compatriots of the German menace, wrote:

> the tragedy which has recently occurred at Sarajevo [the murder by a young Serb of the Austrian Archduke Franz Ferdinand] will, I hope, not lead to any further complications.

Curiously enough, Britain's principal foe, the German Emperor, took much the same view and departed for his annual cruise in Norwegian waters. Both men were wrong and, when an urgent telegram on 29 July told the German Ambassador in Vienna that

'Germany must decline to be irresponsibly dragged into a world war', it was too late. Austria had declared war on Serbia the day before and, on the 29th, Russia initiated the fatal countdown. She began her mobilisation and the First World War could no longer be stopped.[21]

Before a true surprise attack the warning signal may well be absent, but there is more than one way of misreading its presence in a confused situation. On 22 November 1963, when President Kennedy (thirteen months earlier the protagonist in the most acute Super Power crisis of the nuclear era) was assassinated by an ex-Communist who had recently returned from the Soviet Union with his Russian wife, the United State Secretary of Defense and the Joint Chiefs of Staff alerted every US military base throughout the world within an hour. This had no known influence on the main international repercussion of the President's death: the unprecedented number of Heads of State and Government who insisted on attending his funeral. For all its brightness that red signal had been a false alarm.

An alert seldom does much harm and any apparent warning deserves prompt and careful consideration. Admiral Watkins goes a step further. He emphasises that the success of the Maritime Strategy will depend on 'speed and decisiveness in national decisionmaking.' This is partly the traditional exhortation of the military to the political leader, partly the appropriate response to a surprise attack. In a confused situation, where time is needed to assemble and analyse the facts, it can be just as dangerous to act too soon as too late. Of course, navies are more flexible, more withdrawable than armies, but the first phase of the Maritime Strategy does have one feature in common with the continental mobilisations of 1914: it is liable to prompt a response.

Admiral Watkins assumes, as do other American writers, that the Soviet Navy would withdraw from the oceans to await in their coastal bastions the outcome of the political crisis and of American manoeuvres. They may be right. The analogy *Pravda* tried to draw in September 1986, when there was no crisis, just normal tension, may have been a rhetorical rather than a serious expansion of earlier comments by Admiral Chernavin (the Soviet Commander-in-Chief):

the US fleet is on manoeuvres in the immediate vicinity of the Soviet Union – from the Northern Sea and the Baltic to the Far East. Of course these 'shows of muscle' do not frighten our country. But . . . what would happen if the Warsaw Pact countries mounted similar manoeuvres around the United States?'[22]

Military men, naval officers not least, often expect their opponents to behave in a rational manner. Battle should only be sought and, if there is an alternative, accepted, if the circumstances are favourable. Such calculations can be misleading. Hitler sometimes had to override his generals, but, by 1938, years of success justified the belief that the British and French would continue to give way and, if they did not, would easily be defeated. Chamberlain's guarantee to Poland in the spring of 1939, his declaration of war in the autumn, were, as even Churchill pointed out, irrational acts. So was Britain's failure in 1940 to imitate the French surrender. Hitler's belief that he could conquer Russia in 1941, on the other hand, was quite rational (the British Chiefs of Staff were of the same opinion) even if he was unreasonably obstinate in refusing the cheap insurance of equipping his armies for a Russian winter. Again in 1941 some Japanese admirals actually expected to lose a war against the United States, but saw no way of avoiding one.

Historical analogy is an argument that can be so turned and twisted to suit the needs of the user that it is not always convincing. What other people once did, in different circumstances and in another era, may not prove much. But we do have one fairly recent example of a dangerous confrontation between American and Russian naval forces during an international crisis. On 6 October 1973 Egypt and Syria made a surprise attack on Israel. A week later both Super Powers began to resupply their respective clients and to reinforce their own naval strength in the Mediterranean. Diplomatically, however, they were able to cooperate in promoting a ceasefire between Egypt and Israel. Only when this collapsed did the Super Power relationship move into crisis: the Soviet proposal on 24 October to send troops to enforce the ceasefire; the declaration on 25 October of a military alert (DEFCON 3) for American forces everywhere: menacing Soviet naval manoeuvres against American carriers in the Mediterranean between 26 and 30 October. Soviet naval strength in the Mediterranean was continuously increased until 31 October, when the worst of the crisis was over, but even the gradual decline that then began left the Soviet Fifth Eskadra with twice the number of ships on 6 November that there had been on 6 October.[23]

Precedent is not proof. If, in some future international crisis, the United States Navy were to undertake the forward deployment envisaged as the first phase of the Maritime Strategy, the Soviet Navy would not necessarily respond as it did in 1973. Even if confrontation took place, whoever was then US Chief of Naval Operations might have reason for greater confidence in the outcome than Admiral Moorer, who reported:

> Victory in a Mediterranean encounter in 1973 would have depended on which navy struck first and a variety of other factors. Victory would have depended on the type of scenario which occurred.[24]

Initiating the first phase of the Maritime Strategy might, as Admiral Watkins argues, 'enhance deterrence at the brink of war'. It might also lead rather rapidly to confrontation, to conflict, to escalation into nuclear, even total war. What happened would depend, in Admiral Moorer's words, 'on the type of scenario which occurred'.

THE BEST-LAID PLANS

As the received doctrine of the world's leading navy the Maritime Strategy has to be taken seriously. The idea of early forward deployment, for instance, goes some way towards meeting Field-Marshal Lord Carver's objection to the previous strategy of protecting transatlantic reinforcement of the Central Front:

> Unless the reinforcements and supplies reach this side of the Atlantic before hostilities start . . . then I have not much hope, whether they come by air or sea, that they will be very relevant to the situation.[25]

If the Maritime Strategy works, Russian attack submarines will be kept in home-waters to cope with the American battle-groups.

Wars, however, seldom match the plans made for them beforehand. Guessing how long the fighting will last, for instance, is notoriously prone to error. In 1914 the Schlieffen Plan did not bring Germany victory in the promised six weeks, but inaugurated four years of trench warfare. Iran would probably not have been invaded in 1980 if Iraqui leaders had imagined that, seven years later, they would still be fighting and the issue in doubt. And on land one does usually have some idea where the war will be fought. At sea it might be almost anywhere in the northern hemisphere. In December 1984, for instance, 100 Soviet aircraft were scrambled when two US battle-groups, including the aircraft carriers CARL VINSON and MIDWAY, sailed within 50 miles of Vladivostok. Between the Super Powers, because of the extent and approximate parity of their nuclear armament, war would be a more than usually open-ended undertaking.

Naturally it is not enough merely to echo Gorbachev and Reagan by agreeing 'that a nuclear war cannot be won and must never be fought'. Even Hitler could talk of 'the uselessness and horror of war'.[26] If peace is to be maintained, the politicians and admirals of both sides must strike a balance between defence and deterrence, on the one hand, and menace and provocation on the other. Naturally it was as foolish for the Americans to be caught napping at Pearl Harbor in 1941 as it was for the Russians at Port Arthur in 1904. But it may be rash to go to the opposite extreme and start what soldiers used to call 'the approach march to contact' before war has even begun. If, that is, one actually wants to preserve the peace.

On 15 May 1967, for instance, the armed forces of Egypt and her Arab allies began a forward deployment against Israel. Although accompanied by much of the bellicose talk that may also be heard, in time of crisis, from both Moscow and Washington, the manoeuvres of Arab forces were conducted within their own borders. There were even legal pretexts to support Egypt's claim on 22 May to have closed the Straits of Tiran. On 5 June, while a state of nominal peace still obtained, the Israeli Air Force executed a pre-emptive strike and the ensuing war was won in six days. In the United States at least the Israeli action has since been generally approved.

A similar Soviet reaction to Phase I of the Maritime Strategy would presumably be less successful, but would it be wholly implausible? As a deterrent to nuclear war the risks inherent in the Maritime Strategy, indeed in any strategy of preliminary forward deployment, are considerable: the equivalent, perhaps, of fighting fire with fire. Some American critics – the later 1980s saw a running debate in the United States over the Maritime Strategy – argue that the Russians would have a stronger incentive still:

Nuclear war at sea offers overwhelming advantages to the Soviets . . . the vulnerability of the US Navy increases by an order of magnitude if it must fight a nuclear war in Soviet waters.[27]

There is thus less than general agreement that the Maritime Strategy would win the war it might provoke.

2 Limited War at Sea

Soviet military doctrine also recognises the possibility of local wars arising, which will be conducted without the use of nuclear weapons.

In all these wars Soviet military doctrine assigns an important role to the armed struggle at sea. – ADMIRAL STALBO[1]

Limited war means to us that our target list has limits, our ordnance loadout has limits, our rules of engagement have limits, but . . . *not* . . . our personal obligations as fighting men. – COMMANDER JAMES B. STOCKDALE[2]

THE NATURE OF LIMITED WAR

So much has been written about limited war that the failure to agree on a definition is as understandable as it is regrettable. There is a tendency, for instance, to approach the subject from the rather special standpoint of the Super Powers. This not only engenders talk of 'limited' nuclear wars and of the 'inevitable' tendency of local wars to escalate, but allows some writers to envisage a quarter of a million men and three aircraft carrier battle-groups as an appropriate force for limited war.[3] Other American writers even want to see 1000 men killed before they will count a conflict as any kind of war at all.[4] Readers with greater personal experience may be willing to accept a less stringent test. Moreover these criteria might actually exclude the only naval war of our time: one estimate puts the total killed in and around the Falklands in 1982 at 907.[5]

It is not the number of casualties, the duration, the intensity of the fighting, the weapons or the tactics employed that determines whether or not a war is limited. This is a political concept. Wars are limited in much the same way that companies, irrespective of their size or resources, are limited. What is limited is the liability of the participating states. Naturally this is rather a fuzzy, subjective distinction. It works well enough at the extremes. The Second World War, for instance, was not limited. If the Germans and Japanese had won, various states would have disappeared from the map, certain peoples suffered a degree of genocide. Even the Allies demanded unconditional surrender, redrew frontiers, put captured enemy leaders to death, divided states, shuffled populations. The Falklands War of 1982 merely restored in June the status quo disturbed in April.

16

In between those extremes, even between these dates, there have been many wars about which opinions may legitimately differ. Naturally it is always easier for neutrals to regard a war as limited, but states, even nations, engaged in combat may disagree as much about the character of their war as about everything else. The Israelis had some cause to believe that only victory could preserve their national existence in 1948, in 1967 and in 1973. The Arab states that were their enemies neither experienced nor needed to expect much difficulty in surviving defeat. War in Vietnam looked much more limited in Washington than it ever did on the spot. War is limited, as beauty exists, in the eye of the beholder.

The political importance of this sliding scale from total war to violent peace transcends the deplorable absence of precision or objectivity in its gradations. Since 1946, when German leaders were hung at Nürnberg for waging a war of aggression, none of the wars subsequently fought – 25 is at the low end of the range of estimates – has ever been formally declared. With the loss of that convenient touchstone, war, let alone limited war, has become rather hard to identify. Casualties are not a useful criterion. Argentina's generals, for instance, are supposed to have killed between 7000 and 15 000 of their countrymen during the so-called 'dirty war' of the late 1970s, but only 225 members of the British armed forces in 1982. Between 1965 and 1973, 46 226 American servicemen were killed in the Vietnam War. Total Vietnamese deaths are estimated at well over a million,[6] but the Pol Pot regime in Cambodia is supposed to have killed at least a million of its own countrymen between 1977 and 1979 – after that war was officially over. In the world as a whole since 1945 more blood has been shed, more atrocities perpetrated, more destruction inflicted within nation-states than between them.

Definitions have to be arbitrary. War is a violent conflict between states in which policy is determined more by the desire to inflict injury than by the hope of positive reward. Such a war is limited in the eyes of a government able to envisage worse outcomes than failure to achieve victory. For instance, an inconclusive end to the war, even the acceptance of defeat on negotiated terms, may be considered better than extension of the battlefield, particularly to the metropolitan territory; than the belligerent intervention of third parties; than various kinds of escalation; than exceeding a supposedly tolerable level of loss; than incurring an open-ended risk. Political perceptions of this kind are seldom quantifiable, but they often have a significant influence on the way wars are conducted.

WARS WHEN NAVIES WERE NEEDED

It is at least arguable that all the wars since 1945 have been limited. In most of them what determined the outcome was the fighting on land, but Israel's initial air strike decided the Six Day War in 1967. Until 1982 it was never from combat at sea that the victor emerged. In some of these wars a successful naval contribution was nevertheless essential, because, for at least one side, the theatre of operations was overseas. That was the case in Korea (1950–53), a country divided after the Second World War into a Communist North recognised by China as well as by the Soviet Union, and an anti-Communist South recognised by the United States and its allies.

Both Korean governments wanted to reunite Korea under their own control, but the Northern rulers struck first, invading the South with an army of more than seven divisions on 25 June 1950. Because the Soviet Union had earlier withdrawn from the Security Council in protest at the exclusion of China, the United States was able to obtain the endorsement of the United Nations for the decision to give military assistance to the South. Although the Supreme Commander was American (initially General MacArthur) as were most of the non-Korean forces under his command, the opponents of North Korea were nominally the United Nations.

Of every seven fighting men of the United Nations in Korea six had come by ship, as had the bulk of their supplies. The necessary command of the sea was assured by the US Seventh Fleet, assisted by warships from Australia and New Zealand and – although this war had nothing to do with the North Atlantic Alliance – by more NATO navies than have ever fought together on any other occasion. Having disposed of the few North Korean torpedo boats in July 1950, the navies of the United Nations maintained an effective blockade of North Korea against seaborne supplies from China or Russia until the end of the war. Air strikes also began in July 1950: from the carriers USS VALLEY FORGE and HMS TRIUMPH. In September the allied navies participated in a successful amphibious landing at Inchon. As the ground war raged up and down the Korean peninsula, naval forces (including the American battleships IOWA, MISSOURI, NEW JERSEY and WISCONSIN) gave fire support, undertook lesser amphibious operations and provided the sense of ultimate reassurance often needed by those ashore.[7]

Two important lessons learnt in Korea helped to keep subsequent wars limited. Both were derivatives of the saying attributed to

Clemenceau that war is too serious a matter to be left to the military. The first had to be rubbed home by Chinese intervention after American troops had advanced into North Korea: tactical advantage can be too dearly purchased if it provokes a wider war. After a moment's hesitation President Truman, perhaps assisted by a visit from the British Prime Minister, Attlee, decided the second on his own: using nuclear weapons was too big a risk. Neither form of self-restraint has always been popular with the men who fought and risked their lives in later wars, but the second has so far been observed. In the few cases when the first lesson has been ignored (the US invasion of Cambodia in 1970, for instance) the results have been regrettable.

Naval participation was no less essential in the abortive Anglo-French operation at Suez in 1956, which had been provoked by Egypt's earlier nationalisation of the Suez Canal. The main assault on Egypt was seaborne, covered and supported by a substantial fleet, including the aircraft carriers ALBION, ARROMANCHES, BULWARK, EAGLE, LAFAYETTE, OCEAN and THESEUS. Planes from the first five of these carriers attacked targets ashore, those from the ARROMANCHES also disposing of an Egyptian destroyer. The British cruiser NEWFOUND-LAND sank the Egyptian frigate DOMIAT by gunfire. The main landing on 6 November at Port Said was covered by naval gunfire and helicopters also brought commandos ashore from OCEAN and THESEUS.

Although the assault went well, Operation Musketeer, as it was called, was a political disaster from impulsive conception through delay and inter-allied disagreement to premature termination. It revealed grave defects in the organisation, particularly the readiness for action at short notice, of both British and French forces. If it had to be attempted at all, however, navies were needed and, in adverse circumstances mainly not of their own making, they did not do too badly. It was not their fault that this undoubtedly limited war ended ignominiously after only seven days of fighting on 6 November, even if the last British and French forces did not leave Egypt before 22 December.[8]

No end can yet be predicted for the fighting in Indochina and not everyone agrees when it began, originally over the disputed succession to French rule in Indochina. One possible date is 6 March 1946, when the French cruiser EMILE BERTIN opened fire at Haiphong on the Chinese troops who had earlier moved into North Vietnam. They withdrew and did not return in force until 1979. Many other nations fought in Indochina during the years between but mostly on land and in the air. Naturally first the French, then the Americans and their allies had to arrive by sea and to be supplied by sea. In the later years of the American war Russian aid to North Vietnam also came by sea, which was why President Nixon decided in May 1972 to mine Haiphong and other ports, thus interrupting the flow of supplies without a direct confrontation with the Soviet Union.

The United States Navy were involved in many ways. It was a patrol in the Gulf of Tonkin by two American destroyers – MADDOX and C. TURNER JOY – in August 1964 that provided President Johnson with an excuse for committing American forces to combat in Vietnam.[9] When that phase of the war had reached its disastrous end with the capture of Saigon by North Vietnamese forces in April 1975, five carriers of the Seventh Fleet evacuated the last Americans. In between the US Navy had done the usual blockading and bombarding, also organising, from April 1968 onwards, the Mobile Riverine Force: improvised gunboats patrolling the Mekong Delta. The battleship NEW JERSEY again emerged to shell targets ashore. Naval activity was nevertheless only ancillary, as it remained in the fighting of later years among Cambodians, Chinese and Vietnamese.

War is always a barbarity and the war in Indochina has been worse than most wars in the second half of our century. It has gone on so long, caused so much suffering, and has profited none of the combatant nations. It is a relief to turn from such an unmitigated tragedy to confrontation with Indonesia, a war that lasted just over three-and-a-half years, killed under 1000, ended on 11 August 1966 and has not since been renewed. It was another war of imperial succession and it got its peculiar name because President Sukarno, the autocratic ruler of Indonesia, had declared his intention of 'confronting' (even he fought shy of the word 'war') the federation of Malaysia. This was a state the British had decided to form in 1963 by uniting their remaining colonies and protectorates in South East Asia with already independent Malaya. Sukarno, however, wanted for himself the three British territories along the northern coast of Borneo (the rest of the island was already Indonesian): Sarawak, Brunei and British North Borneo.

The Indonesian strategy of subversion and infiltration, which had earlier worked well in their struggle for independence from the Dutch, now failed them for reasons that were primarily political. They had too few sympathisers in Malaysia and were forced to rely mainly on their own military efforts. Up to 17 000 Commonwealth troops (the British making the largest single contribution) had to be deployed in Borneo against Indonesian overland infiltration and nearly as many in mainland Malaya and Singapore, where units from Malaya, Singapore, Australia and New Zealand were more prominent.

The British Far East Fleet, which had to deter Indonesian warships from attempting a sortie, to intercept seaborne raiding parties and to ensure the safety of maritime communications, had as many as 80 ships. They included the aircraft carriers VICTORIOUS and CENTAUR, together with ALBION and BULWARK, these last converted since Suez to commando carriers. They and their helicopters had a more active role than the strike carriers, for the Indonesian navy prudently posed no challenge and the British conception of this limited war had no place for the idea of trying to bomb civilians into national surrender.[10]

Of course, the British and the peoples of Malaysia were lucky: Indonesian unity was the first to crack and it was Sukarno's deposition by his own generals that brought the war to an end. But victory rewarded Malaysia (and subsequent events suggest the reward was real) only because they and their Commonwealth allies had held out meanwhile. To which endurance, mainly the achievement of soldiers, there had to be a naval contribution. Borneo is an island.

THE OPTIONAL USE OF NAVIES

In the 1950s, 1960s and 1970s, these were the wars in which navies were essential to those belligerents who had to send their soldiers overseas to fight. In other wars of this period the opposing armies and their supporting aircraft had only a land frontier to cross. When warships also fought one another, it was more because they existed than because they were needed. In Israel's running war with her Arab neighbours there were occasional instances of combat at sea. On 31 October 1956 an Egyptian destroyer, the IBRAHIM AL-AWAL, shelled installations at Haifa and was captured by the Israelis, who used her against Port Said in 1967. There and elsewhere shots were exchanged between vessels of the Israeli and Egyptian navies. October 1973 saw more activity. Israeli missile-armed fast attack craft managed to sink a number of their Egyptian and Syrian opponents and to bombard enemy ports. As in 1967 neither these encounters nor the blockade of Israel proclaimed by Egypt made any difference to the outcome of a war decided on land and in the air.

In the turbulent history of the Middle East since 1945 navies

engaged in actual war have had less impact on the course of events –
the Anglo-French fleet in the Suez War is only a partial exception –
than the non-belligerent navies confronting one another or manifesting a presence or posing a threat or even making one of the forcible
interventions of violent peace.

Of course, those non-belligerents included the United States Sixth
Fleet, the Soviet Mediterranean Squadron, on occasion sizeable
French or British forces with the odd aircraft carrier. In 1967, for
instance, the devastating attack on Egypt by the Israeli Air Force
was, with deliberate mendacity, blamed by Nasser, then the ruler of
Egypt, on British and American aircraft. In fact, HMS VICTORIOUS and
HMS HERMES were both out of range: at Malta and Aden respectively.
But the dominant influence was always that of the US Sixth Fleet,
whose confrontation in October 1973 by the Soviet Mediterranean
Squadron marked the second most serious Super Power crisis since
1945 and was far more important, not only to the rest of the world,
but even to Israel and the Arabs than anything the navies of the
actual belligerents could attempt.

It was again the movements of neutral navies that attracted most
attention during the brief Indo-Pakistan War of December 1971, a
limited war that cost Pakistan a province with nearly twice the
population of England. The British Far East Fleet, then withdrawing
from Singapore, happened to be crossing the Indian Ocean en route
for the Persian Gulf. The American Task Force 74 (including the
attack carrier ENTERPRISE) was deliberately and with diplomatic intent
ordered into that ocean. Soviet naval detachments shadowed both
the British carrier EAGLE in the west and the American ENTERPRISE in
the east. None of these ships actually did anything and the exploits
of the Indian and Pakistani navies had less influence on events ashore
than some Indian writers have suggested.

The fourteen days the war lasted were not really enough for even
the successful Indian blockade of Eastern Pakistan to bite to the
bone. Aircraft from the Indian carrier VIKRANT attacked enemy
airfields and a couple of ships on either side were sunk or damaged
in brief encounters in the Arabian Sea. Neutral merchant vessels
fared almost as badly, the Liberian tanker VENUS CHALLENGER, for
instance, being sunk (probably by a Styx missile from an Indian OSA-
class fast-attack-craft) with all her crew. Her fate, no less than that
of the British ship HARMATTAN or the Greek GULF STAR may not even
have been intended. If either side in 1971 had possessed no navy,
the result of the war would scarcely have been other than it was.

The latest war (it is still in progress) in which the use of navies was optional began on 23 September 1980 between Iran and Iraq. It does not slot easily into any of the established categories. The recurrent intensity of the fighting, the bombing of civilians by both sides, the alleged use of poison gas by Iraq, the stiff peace terms demanded by Iran, the attacks each belligerent has made on neutral shipping in the Persian Gulf: these are features that even cast some doubt on the limited character of the war. Perhaps Israel, presumably acting quite independently, did well to bomb the Iraqui nuclear reactor in June 1981. Nevertheless, the Iraquis have more than once sought a negotiated end to the war they started and the Iranians have – so far and rather narrowly – refrained from widening it, in spite of the important economic assistance given to Iraq by other Gulf States. Nor has Iran implemented her repeated threat to close the Straits of Hormuz to shipping, in spite of the many Iraqui air attacks on tankers exporting Iranian oil.

Closing the Straits, of course, might well hurt Iran as much or more than Iraq, whose pipelines across Turkey and Saudi Arabia provide alternative outlets for oil exports. Moreover, it might provoke outside intervention, particularly by the United States, whose warships have been patrolling – mostly outside, often at the mouth of, latterly well inside the Persian Gulf – for many years. Indeed, it is not obvious that the attacks made by both sides on neutral shipping in the Gulf have brought either more advantage than could have been expected from tacit agreement to refrain from such extension of the war.

The International Institute for Strategic Studies, on the other hand, has argued that Iraq, conscious that Iran had the edge in the land-fighting, actually wanted to widen the war and, in 1984, intensified their campaign against tankers in the hope of provoking Iran into rash action that would have that result.[11] So far Iran has preferred to retaliate against merchant ships serving Iraq or her Arab supporters in the Gulf. In January 1987 the Chairman of the International Chamber of Shipping complained, in a letter to *The Times*, that nearly 200 ships had been attacked, over 100 seafarers killed and 30 ships sunk. Most of these attacks were made by the aircraft of the two belligerents. The Iranian Navy, which enjoyed the advantage at sea, was more often reported as stopping and searching ships suspected of carrying cargo destined for Iraq (16 in 1985, for instance). In January and February 1987, however, Iranian frigates fired missiles at ships bound for Kuwait. Fortunately the Italian missiles were rather elderly and did not explode.[12] The unidentified patrol boats that attacked the Soviet cargo ship IVAN KOROTEYEV in May 1987 are likely also to have been Iranian – perhaps crewed by the Revolutionary Guards.[13]

Firm conclusions concerning a war still in progress and on which information has always been scanty would be premature. But it does seem arguable that the war has so far been limited, perhaps mainly because neither belligerent could escalate or extend it, as at least one of them may occasionally have wished. Even when more is known of naval activities on either side – the Iranian Navy, for instance, is supposed to have destroyed coastal oil installations in Iraq on 24 September 1980 – these are unlikely to seem significant by comparison with those of the opposing armies and air forces. Only if action is eventually taken by the watching warships of the major naval powers (an issue discussed in Chapter 5) will this important war (the total killed is unreliably said to approach a million) deserve a place in naval history.

THE NAVAL WAR

Of course, Operation Rosario was not meant to start any kind of war. The Argentine Task Force 40, comprising the tank landing ship CABO SAN ANTONIO, the destroyers SANTISIMA TRINIDAD and HERCULES, the frigates DRUMMOND and GRANVILLE, as well as other vessels, had a different mission: 'el uso o amenaza de uso del poder naval limitado, no entendido como acta de guerra, para asegurarse ventaja.'[14] That was how, in 1977, gunboat diplomacy was defined in a translation commissioned by the Centro Naval de Buenos Aires from the English original: 'the use or threat of limited naval force, otherwise than as an act of war, in order to secure advantage'. Rosario was to be a simple amphibious operation, a definitive use of limited naval force which the victim could not resist and in which he would thus have to acquiesce.

On 2 April 1982 the Argentine marines landed by Task Force 40 at Port Stanley, capital of the Falkland Islands, outnumbered the defenders (also marines) by ten to one, had armoured vehicles, were reinforced by air and enjoyed ample fire-support. It did not take them long and probably cost them only 20 to 30 casualties to overcome British resistance and secure a surrender. Soon the occupation of key points elsewhere brought the whole of the Falkland Islands under the control of Argentina, who deployed more troops in their newly-conquered territory than there were islanders. If that had been the end of the affair, if British indignation had found a sufficient outlet in oratory, in United Nations resolutions, even in economic sanctions, Operation Rosario would have been accounted a textbook triumph of gunboat diplomacy.

As Admiral Anaya, the Commander-in-Chief of the Argentine Navy should have known, victims sometimes reciprocate the violence they have been too feckless to prevent or resist. Even the most effective use of limited naval force will occasionally escalate into the unintended brutality of war. The conduct of successive British governments; their reductions – accomplished or announced – in the strength of the Royal Navy; the long absence of any effective defences in the Falkland Islands; the sheer distance between Portsmouth and Port Stanley: these were only some of the plausible arguments Admiral Anaya and his colleagues in the Argentine Junta could have employed to discredit the risk of a forcible British response. Their surprise, when it happened, was widely echoed, even in Britain itself.

It was a rare example, not matched since the Pacific conflict of 1941–5, of an essentially naval war. Whereas Argentina might possibly, if politically prepared for war, have seized the islands, albeit with greater violence and more casualties, by a purely airborne operation, this was never an option for Britain – nearly 8000 miles away. In the words of Admiral Sir Henry Leach, then, as First Sea Lord, the professional head of the British navy: 'there was no conceivable means of any UK agency doing anything about it unless they were got there by the Navy and protected by the Navy when they got there.'[15]

At such a distance the naval response could naturally not be immediate, though the four-week interval between the Argentine landing and the first British naval bombardment showed a marked improvement on Operation Musketeer in 1956. Moreover, the necessarily lengthy business of deploying the British task force (the aircraft carriers HERMES and INVINCIBLE sailed from Portsmouth on 5 April, but attacked Argentine forces at Port Stanley only on 1 May) had its diplomatic advantages. There was ample time, as the United States, the United Nations and others attempted mediation, for Britain to appear reasonable and Argentina to emerge as intransigent. As one sailing followed another, as British ships were reported at the midpoint of Ascension Island, when the Antarctic outpost of South Georgia was repossessed on 25 April, it became obvious that Britain meant business. From Buenos Aires, where the junta had more to fear from their own people than from the British, no reasonable response could be expected, but Britain's gradual, diplomatically flexible approach to limited war made a better impression in the United States and helped to shift American attitudes from dispassionate mediation to tacit support.

By 1 May, when hostilities began at Port Stanley, Argentina had rejected the last American compromise proposal and President Reagan had expressed support for Britain (who had already received discreet American logistic assistance). Other intermediaries were then employed in seeking some basis for a negotiated settlement, but nothing emerged to suggest a serious prospect of escaping the need to repossess the islands. The first step – dominating the air and sea around the islands – was the job of the ships and carrier-borne aircraft commanded by Rear-Admiral Woodward. Some soulless bureaucrat, instead of calling them the Falklands Fleet or the South Atlantic Squadron, gave them a computerised dog-tag: Task Unit 318.1.[16] Even Woodward's peacetime command had enjoyed the more dignified and British title of First Flotilla.

Nearly three weeks were devoted to the bombardment (from both air and sea) of Argentine positions ashore, to reconnaissance, to the discouragement of reinforcement from the mainland and to preparations for the eventual landing of ground forces. The opposition encountered was all from the air. The Argentine Navy, admittedly, had sent out an aircraft carrier, a cruiser, 7 destroyers and 3 frigates on 27 April, but lack of a favourable wind prevented the carrier VEINTICINCO DE MAYO from launching an air strike against the British task-force on the morning of 2 May.[17] Later that day the British submarine CONQUEROR sank the cruiser BELGRANO, thereby effectively deterring any further interference by Argentine warships in the course of the war. On 4 May, however, land-based aircraft of the Argentine Navy successfully attacked the British destroyer SHEFFIELD with an Exocet missile. SHEFFIELD had to be abandoned and sank six days later.

These events were only a prelude to the Navy's most important and most dangerous task: protecting against air attack from the Argentine mainland the disembarkation of British ground forces in San Carlos Water from 21 May onwards. The frigates ANTELOPE and ARDENT were sunk, as was the destroyer COVENTRY. ANTRIM, ARGONAUT, BRILLIANT and BROADSWORD were damaged. But the troops were landed without serious loss and the ships that had carried them, including the 45 000-ton liner CANBERRA, survived. The worst logistic casualty, the heavily-laden supply ship ATLANTIC CONVEYOR, was lost to another Exocet missile on 25 May when she was well out to sea with the British aircraft carriers. Although the invaluable Harrier aircraft from HERMES and INVINCIBLE played a major part in the defence of the landing area, there were never enough of them to exempt the destroyers and frigates from this perilous duty.

Once the troops ashore had begun their arduous approach march across East Falkland to Port Stanley, the naval role, though still important and often dangerous, took on a more auxiliary character. Where it departed from the pattern of earlier wars – those in Korea and Indochina, for instance – was that air support for the British ground forces still had to come from the carriers. Bombardment from the sea was also more hazardous than formerly: the destroyer GLAMORGAN was damaged and had 13 men killed by an Exocet fired from Stanley on 12 June, only two days before the Argentine forces under General Menéndez capitulated and the war was over.

It had been a limited war, which neither side attempted to extend and in which both spared civilians. For Britain, at least, it had also been an uniquely naval war. It was not just that, as had happened on earlier occasions, a navy was needed to enter the game at all. Even if we only start the clock on 1 May, nearly 4 weeks, more than half the whole war, passed before there was any significant fighting ashore. Until 28 May warships and aircraft operating from warships had borne almost all the British share of the battle. Before that date almost certainly, even after that date probably, the loss of HERMES or INVINCIBLE would have doomed the British campaign. It can even be argued that it was really the Argentine Navy who lost the war Admiral Anaya had done so much to start. A really determined attack on the British carriers – VEINTICINCO DE MAYO had not been located by British submarines when she withdrew on 2 May, before the loss of BELGRANO – might have stopped what the British called Operation Corporate dead in the water.

THE RECORD AND THE PROSPECTS

As the British Ministry of Defence was anxious to emphasise, 'the Falklands Campaign was in many respects unique'.[18] In most limited wars since 1945 armies have been much more important than navies and in many of them navies were not used at all. The world's second largest navy, that of the Soviet Union, never engaged in any kind of war during this period. Nor did the smaller, but still significant navies of the Federal Republic of Germany, of Italy, of Japan or of Spain. Even among actual belligerents perhaps only Argentina, Britain, France and the United States could convincingly assert that recent experience of war proved they needed a navy. In other countries arguments of a different character would be required to refute the suggestion that naval tasks could be divided more economically between the air force in war and some kind of coast guard in peace.

In any society, of course, the organisation of the armed forces tends to conform to the patterns established by national customs and tradition. The long survival – twenty years after the first tank-battle – of horsed cavalry in the British army is a case in point. This instinctive conservatism has to be weighed against the equally impulsive radicalism of some politicians. Even in once-navalist Britain it has been suggested in recent years that rash overseas adventures might best be avoided by renouncing the maintenance of an ocean-going navy. This is the extravagance of opposition, which tends to wither in government, but Defence Ministers of different parties – Duncan Sandys in 1957, Denis Healey in 1966, John Nott in 1981 – have repeatedly demonstrated to British admirals that navies are particularly vulnerable to the more expedient arguments of the economisers and the innovators.

Does the record since 1945 support the view that coastal states still need navies to fight the wars in which events may involve them? This question, which will be further explored in Chapter 9, has one simple answer. Those with interests or positions to defend beyond the seas certainly do, but such nations are now a small and shrinking minority. Countries only concerned to defend their own coasts against seaborne attack might prefer to sacrifice a small navy to strengthen their air force or even, as some countries already do, to let their sailors man coastal artillery or otherwise stand guard ashore. Chinese admirals, for instance, command over 600 tanks. In the closing years of the twentieth century it is no longer obvious that seaborne enemies are always best confronted by ships at sea. It would be a rash prophet who suggested that warships would not be needed in future wars, but a foolish admiral whose case for keeping a navy depended solely on the likelihood of using it in war at sea. The record of the recent past is ambiguous and there are other arguments to be explored.

One of them – the idea that the Super Powers might engage in a limited war at sea – requires rather different assumptions from those underlying the Maritime Strategy. Admiral Watkins, for instance, emphasised that 'the Maritime Strategy is designed to support campaigns in ground theaters of operations both directly and indirectly'.[19] This was only one of the premises which made it so hard to imagine how any war in which the Maritime Strategy was employed could remain limited. But might American and Russian warships fight one another in what Admiral Stalbo called 'local wars'?[20]

It is not too hard to invent a scenario culminating in a naval confrontation in a distant sea and for some cause a little remote from the central quarrel. Civil war in South Africa, for instance, might prompt a doctrine of non-intervention, even an international blockade, which one Super Power supported and the other wished to defy. When the standstill imposed by the Antarctic Treaty of 1959 expires in 1991, the Soviet Union and the United States, who both reserved the right to make claims of their own, might collide in their haste to stake out the southern ice. Could not a distant conflict which posed no threat to the metropolitan territory or the vital interests of either power remain limited?

It is conceivable, but it does not seem very likely. Both navies, after all, are trained and equipped for the battle of the first salvo. If either opens fire, even with conventional weapons, the chances are that ships will quickly be sunk and tension become acute. An immediate resort to negotiation would then surely be the only alternative to escalation. It can scarcely be supposed that the United States and the Soviet Union, if they went on fighting, could imitate Britain and Argentina by confining their hostilities to the South Atlantic. Even an armistice might not be easy to arrange after a naval battle.

So far the Super Powers have managed – sometimes only just – to avoid putting their fraught relationship under too many kinds of strain at a time. When the Soviet Union had to back down in the Cuban Missile Crisis of 1962 or over the Arab–Israeli War in 1973, at least there had been no shooting and no Russian casualties. When two American reconnaissance aircraft, in two incidents separated by an interval of two months, were shot down by Soviet forces in 1960, it could at least be argued that they had only succumbed to the occupational hazards of espionage.

The US warships that sniff round Soviet bases – in May 1987 it was the 10000-ton nuclear-propelled cruiser ARKANSAS off the Kamchatka peninsula – have so far escaped unscathed. In 1987 both American and Russian ships were attacked in the Persian Gulf – but by third parties. The losses of a limited war might perhaps be accepted by both sides if the outcome of their confrontation left the prestige of each intact. But could it? Would anyone confidently expect such a result?

Limited war at sea between a Super Power and a lesser power, or between two lesser powers, is easier to imagine. It could happen, as did some of the wars mentioned in this chapter, because ground forces were sent beyond the seas to fight on land. Such a war might also be the result, as was the Falklands War of 1982, of a misconceived effort at gunboat diplomacy. Libya and Iran are states which could conceivably react to some future application of limited naval force by the United States in a manner that would escalate the conflict into actual war. A particularly dangerous situation might develop if Iran defeated Iraq, and other Gulf States then sought the protection of the US Navy.

At a lower level, if the rivalry of Argentina and Chile ever gets out of hand, the sea might provide a more convenient battleground than the high passes of the Andean mountains. New causes for limited war at sea might even emerge from such issues as the control of pollution, the policing of exclusive economic zones, the mining of the seabed or the closure, complete or partial, of international straits. Of course, all this is really the domain of gunboat diplomacy, but accidents, as Admiral Anaya discovered, do occasionally happen.

For over forty years the incidence of war at sea has been much lower than on land. There is no obvious reason why the ratio should alter in future. It was the surging era of European expansion into the outer world that saw the heyday of navies and of naval war. If we attack our canvas with a broad and generous brush, embracing means as well as motive, we may say it lasted from the Armada in 1588 to Tsushima in 1905. These were the centuries in which the fate of empires could turn on a battle at sea. The two world wars that followed were of an amplitude that transcended even the important naval campaigns they included, but which concerned only a minority of the participants. A third could, at least in theory, be fought with strategic submarines making the only naval contribution of any significance.

Many nations, of course, keep navies today without believing that they have anything to gain from war at sea, but merely because they might need a navy if attacked. Sweden, for instance, has not fought any kind of war since 1809 and, in the twentieth century, war for the Spanish Navy has meant civil war. Most naval officers nevertheless tend to regard the employment of their ships in time of peace, even of violent peace, as less important, less central to the purpose of their professional lives, than their role in war. This is understandable, but it is only an act of faith. Very few people in the German, Italian, Japanese, Russian or Spanish navies – indeed, in most of the world's navies – have any experience of war at sea. Those who do have such experience are in a minority even in the American, Argentinian, British, Chinese and French navies. We may reasonably hope, though we cannot be confident, that most of the world's sailors will complete their careers without being ordered to open fire in an international war. This need not, as subsequent chapters will endeavour to demonstrate, detract from the utility of their functions. In the final decades of the twentieth century there remain other and more frequent uses for navies.

3 Proxy War at Sea

Internationalism and its ideals of solidarity and fraternity among peoples form the beautiful essence of Marxism-Leninism. Without internationalism the Cuban revolution wouldn't even exist. Being internationalists is one way of paying our debt to humanity. . . . our military cooperation with Angola and Ethiopia was not something new. Cuban soldiers went to the sister republic of Algeria in 1963 to support it against foreign aggression when, in the months following the victory of its heroic struggle for independence, attempts were made to grab a part of its territory. Cuban soldiers went to Syria in 1973 when that country requested our help right after the last war waged against the Zionist aggressors. Cuban fighters fought and died to help free Guinea-Bissau and Angola from Portuguese colonialism – CASTRO[1]

The idea of proxy war was so overworked during the 1950s, particularly in the United States, that the concept later fell into greater academic disrepute than it deserved. Getting other people to do the fighting is, after all, the traditional practice of the richer nations. In the eighteenth century, England and France employed soldiers from many different European countries, usually paying the ruler for the use of his subjects. In the nineteenth and twentieth centuries the imperial powers could recruit from their colonies, but the British also enlisted, as they and the Indians do to this day, Gurkha soldiers from independent Nepal. This is now something of an exception, for the triumph of nationalism has engendered widespread hostility, right across the political spectrum, to the ancient profession of mercenary soldiering. Governments desirous of having their fighting done by others must nowadays enlist states rather than individuals and, even if some money still passes to rulers, pay a predominantly political price.

A political price, of course, is not paid in a freely negotiable currency at the command of mere wealth. Before one government can hire another, their purposes must be at least compatible. When they paid their 'debt to humanity' in Africa and the Middle East, Cuban soldiers were serving the needs of the Soviet Union and discharging some of the obligations Cuba had incurred. They were also manifesting a specifically Cuban aspiration not confined to Castro himself: to a leading role in the Third World. They would not have fought, however rewarded, for the United States, not even for the arguably Marxist-Leninist Chinese, whom Castro had denounced.

Even a political price must nevertheless be negotiated. In the first shock of realising, as the 1940s gave way to the 1950s, that Communism had enabled the Soviet Government to exercise a special kind of influence in certain foreign countries, there was a tendency among Western politicians, of both the practising and the theorising kinds, to exaggerate the potency of this new drug they themselves could not buy. Dulles, later US Secretary of State, wrote in 1950 of the Soviet Union and China as having:

a comprehensive program . . . designed as a present phase to eliminate all Western influence on the Asiatic mainland, and probably also in relation to the islands of Japan, Formosa, the Philippines and Indonesia.

Communist success in the then recently completed Chinese revolution and Communist activities in Indochina, the Philippines and Malaya, no less than the attack on South Korea, were:

all part of a single pattern of violence planned and plotted for twenty-five years and finally brought to a consummation of fighting and disorder.[2]

That was not, perhaps, a misrepresentation of Russian dreams – as early as 1921 Stalin had called for 'all necessary measures to strengthen the national liberation movements in the East'[3] – but it was a considerable exaggeration of their abilities. Dulles was not alone. In the same year Dean Rusk, then Deputy Under-Secretary of State in Washington, described the Chinese government headed by Mao Tse-Tung as

a colonial Russian government – a Slavic Manchukuo . . . not Chinese.[4]

The Russians, at least in Stalin's time, sometimes entertained hopes as illusory as American fears. Nowadays there is rather more understanding of the tenacious character, even in weak states, of nationalism.

Nevertheless, both Super Powers, conscious of the extreme danger of direct conflict between themselves, would still prefer to get other people to do their fighting by proxy. Neither has commanded the services of entirely obedient puppets, but each has, at one time or another, received useful assistance from allies or clients. These helpful countries are not always the same. Egypt left the Soviet camp for the American; Ethiopia made an opposite change. In the last forty years the list of the fickle, but not always non-aligned, stretches from Afghanistan to Zimbabwe. A few, even outside the major alliances, have been steadfast, but Cuba (a Soviet client since 1959) and Israel (an American client since 1948) have kept and occasionally manifested wills of their own. The Russians, it has been well said, 'can count on the Cubans in situations where Cuban and Russian interests happen to coincide'.[5] American scholars tend to reject the simplistic view of American politicians that Cuba is only 'the Soviet Union's proxy in Africa'.[6]

In 1987 President Habré of Chad pleased the United States, who had given him some logistic and intelligence backing, by defeating Libyan forces equipped with Soviet weapons. Yet Chad was not a client of the United States, but of France, and even with France relations in the quarter century since independence had often been strained. Habré had reasons of his own for attacking the Libyans and his patrons served his purpose as much as he served theirs. Meanwhile the Gulf War, which neither Super Power had prompted and which neither seemed able to control, was in its seventh year. Americans and Russians, evidently despairing of Iran, appeared at one stage to be competing, a little dubiously, for the uncertain rewards of rescuing Iraq (originally reckoned a Soviet client) from probable defeat. Proxy war is less simple than is sometimes supposed.

Nevertheless, outside powers do often try to profit from conflicts in which they are not themselves directly involved. Even if there is no client to be sustained or acquired, there may be a rival or a rival's satellite to be weakened. Americans and Pakistanis are presumably aware of Kim's advice – 'trust a Brahmin before a snake, and a snake before a harlot, and a harlot before an Afghan'[7] – but they help the mujahidin because that hurts the Russians and *their* Afghan clients. Help, in such cases, is usually logistic. In Afghanistan it does not, but elsewhere it often does, arrive by sea. Soviet ships brought the heavy weapons needed by the Cuban soldiers who flew to both coasts of Africa. Even the combat aircraft the Israelis so desperately needed in October 1973 had to use American carriers as the indispensable staging-point on their flight from the United States.

These carriers, with their escorts, could look after themselves, but cargo ships sometimes need naval protection against the coastal forces of the other belligerent. In 1969 and 1970 Soviet equipment bound for Guinea had been captured by the Portuguese, who also attempted a raid from the neighbouring colony on the capital, Conakry. The Soviet naval patrol that developed into a small but lasting West African squadron began in December 1970.[8] It was no less useful in 1975 and 1976, when Soviet freighters brought aircraft, tanks and other munitions of war for the popular liberation movement (MPLA) in Angola.[9]

So far seaborne supplies from one Super Power to a client have seldom encountered a naval challenge from the other Super Power. In 1954, when the US Navy sought to intercept arms shipments to the Communist government of Guatemala, the cargo ships involved were Swedish or British, not Russian. In October 1962 the Cuban Missile Crisis was so acute that stopping and searching Russian ships on the high seas actually seemed the least dangerous course open to the United States. In 1972 it was considered more prudent to mine North Vietnamese ports (from the air) to prevent the arrival of ships (some of them British) carrying Soviet munitions. But the Soviet freighters resupplying Egypt and Syria in October 1973 did not have to be protected against the US Sixth Fleet, only against Israeli fast attack craft, which sank a Soviet freighter in Tartus harbour before Soviet destroyers were deployed on escort duties. Nor did the Soviet Fifth Eskadra menace American carriers while these ships were maintaining the air-bridge to Israel, but only after the US alert of 25 October.[10]

In 1976, the United States Government considered, as a possible reaction to Russian naval presence off Angola, sending the carrier ENTERPRISE and a task-force to the South Atlantic, but decided against it.[11] They were equally cautious in 1978, on the other side of Africa, when the Soviet Union were transferring their patronage and their seaborne supplies, from Somalia to Ethiopia.[12] In the long war between Iran and Iraq American and Russian warships were constantly in presence in the Gulf, but so far both have shown a mutual circumspection not always observed by the US Navy, once Reagan had become President, off the coasts of metropolitan Russia. The cruiser YORKTOWN and the destroyer CARON, for instance, had drawn sharp Soviet protests by the closeness of their approach to the Crimean peninsula in March 1986. But, when the USS STARK was crippled by a French Exocet in the Gulf in May 1987, the missile had been fired by an Iraqui aircraft. Nobody in Washington blamed the Russians. Instead the Americans, such are the paradoxes of the late twentieth century, threatened Iran and encouraged Kuwait, one of

Iraq's financial backers, to put some of their own merchant ships under the protection of the Stars and Stripes.

So far the sea has played only an ancillary role in proxy war. The main fighting has been on land or in the air over the land. The belligerents have usually been neighbouring states, sometimes factions within a single state. Each has been assisted by an outside power or group of powers. These powers usually try (Cuba is something of an exception) to avoid doing any fighting themselves and often succeed. Instead, they provide supplies, intelligence, advice, technicians (occasionally even such specialised combatants as pilots or missile operators), training and encouragement to their chosen client. Some of the supplies usually come by sea, warships may cover their arrival and occasionally execute encouraging manoeuvres at a safe distance.

For our purposes it does not much matter whose idea the war originally was, whether the combatant is exploiting the coat-holder or vice versa. Client and patron both believe, rightly or wrongly, that victory would be rewarding. When they differ, as they often do, in their notions of what would actually constitute victory, how much it would be worth paying to achieve it or what the concrete rewards might be, they try to obscure these issues as long as they can.

Naturally all this can go disastrously wrong. The classic example is Indochina, where the United States backed a loser in France, found another in South Vietnam, got sucked in themselves and went down to defeat while Russia and China never left the sidelines. By comparison with that débâcle any disappointment in Pretoria at the absence of adequate American backing for the intervention in Angola which South Africa began in 1975 was trifling. In 1987, when the client did all the fighting in Nicaragua but the patron was heavily engaged in Afghanistan, it seemed as if Americans might have learned more from failure in Vietnam than had Russians from success in Africa.

What has hitherto been lacking from the historical record is a proxy war in which the clients fought at sea. This is hardly surprising. All war, as we have already noted, is less frequent at sea, where navies can achieve political ends by the use or threat of limited force not involving actual war. A major power, even a cautious major power, which would shrink from landing a single platoon on foreign soil, will deploy a fleet at sea, knowing it can easily be withdrawn. Gunboat diplomacy sometimes offers a controlled escape at sea from that awkward choice ashore: between inaction and promoting action by an all too autonomous client. Nor are there, among the world's lesser powers, as many ships for hire as there are battalions. It would not be easy to arrange a proxy war at sea.

It might nevertheless be a mistake to suppose it could never be done. In 1982 Britain and Argentina went to war against the advice of the United States and in spite of protracted American efforts to promote a negotiated solution. The Soviet representative on the Security Council disappointed Argentina by abstaining on the resolution calling for the withdrawal of their forces from the Falkland Islands. Nor, once war had begun, does Argentina seem to have received from the Soviet Union even the discreet assistance which the United States then extended to Britain. Those Russian reconnaissance aircraft from Luanda appear to have reported only to Moscow on the southward progress of the British Task Force. Castro warmly embraced the Argentine Foreign Minister at a meeting in Havana, but did not offer any Cuban soldiers to stiffen Argentine forces in the Falklands.[13] The Falklands was not a proxy war.

In slightly different circumstances it could have been. Suppose the junta in Buenos Aires that launched Operation Rosario against the Falklands had been as left-wing as the generals, a few years earlier, in Peru. This allows us to guess that the US Representative to the United Nations would not then have dined with the Argentine Ambassador in Washington on 2 April 1982. The Secretary of State, Al Haig, would not have wasted three weeks seeking a compromise to suit Argentina and save British face. The Task Force would have been assisted by AWACS reconnaissance aircraft; the Soviet Union would have vetoed Resolution 502 in the Security Council; and Tupolev freighters staging through friendly African and South American airfields would have filled the gaps in Argentina's military inventory.

In 1973, if General Pinochet had declined the invitation of the Central Intelligence Agency to rid Chile of President Allende, it is conceivable that the US Government would have encouraged the Argentine Navy to a vigorous pursuit of their country's claims in the Beagle Channel. If that had led to naval war between Argentina and Chile, the left-wing President Allende could surely have counted on Soviet logistic support, even if, ostensibly, this came only from Cuba.

Scenarios, of course, prove nothing. Consider, instead, this list of countries with both navies and potential enemies.

Argentina   Chile
Australia   Indonesia
Brazil   Venezuela

Egypt	Israel
Greece	Turkey
India	Pakistan
Iran	Iraq
Japan	either Korea
Spain	Britain (Gibraltar)

Not all of them will go to war in the future. A few could as conveniently fight on land or in the air as at sea. But in no case is war at sea inconceivable. If such conflicts ever happened, one or two might develop into proxy wars at sea. It is not very probable, but it is not out of the question.

4 The Persistence of Gunboat Diplomacy

Prime Minister has decided that necessary number not (repeat not) of soldiers but of armed police from Singapore with good proportion of white officers should proceed at once in one of HM ships to Pulau Sambu and unless Indonesian reinforcements have already arrived and have restored the situation should land and ensure law and order. – FO TELEGRAM TO SINGAPORE NO. 77, 1 February 1952[1]

We have a flash report from the Joint Reconnaissance Centre indicating a US electronic intelligence ship, the LIBERTY, has been torpedoed in the Mediterranean. – WALT ROSTOW to President Johnson, 8 June 1967[2]

The invasion of Grenada was a treacherous surprise attack . . . presented to the US people as a great victory for Reagan's foreign policy against the socialist camp and the revolutionary movement. – CASTRO, 26 October 1983[3]

War at sea, as surveyed in the preceding chapters, seems unlikely to offer most navies much of a livelihood. If total, war would probably also be terminal. If limited, war may not involve navies at all and, if it does, their role may only be ancillary or even optional. Proxy war at sea is so far the merest hypothesis. Since 1945 only 25 of the world's 105 navies have any shadow of a claim to have fought, even fleetingly, a foreign enemy in war at sea. These navies can nevertheless expect more employment, as can many of the remainder, in time of peace than in future war.

One way in which navies can be employed is often called gunboat diplomacy:

the use or threat of limited naval force, otherwise than as an act of war, in order to secure advantage, or to avert loss, either in the furtherance of an international dispute or else against foreign nationals within the territory or the jurisdiction of their own state.[4]

The political application of limited naval force is a special case of a more widespread practice: coercive diplomacy. Even that is exceptional in the conduct of international relations. States usually find other ways to resolve conflicts of interest or aspiration. Many disputes are avoided or quietly settled by no more than the implicit coercion that obtains between patron and client, or springs from an alliance or prompts the appeasement of sleeping dogs. When resort is had to coercive diplomacy – threatening to do something injurious to the interest of another government unless that government either takes or desists from or refrains from some indicated course of action – it is usually because other expedients are not available or, having been tried, have already failed. A variety of pressures – economic, financial, administrative, propagandist – may then be considered. Armed force, if it is appropriate at all, is the last expedient short of war and that force cannot always be applied by ships.[5]

So limited naval force has never been a routine practice. Today it may even be in less frequent use than in some previous eras. We can safely ignore those antiquarians who like to pretend it is only

> kept alive by the fashion for Victorian prints of British gunboats off Chingwangtao, or of cruisers lying at anchor off West African towns.[6]

No doubt they do not read the newspapers. Arthur Balfour never did.

In the annals of gunboat diplomacy since 1919 there is just one year without an instance. That was 1944, when almost all the world was at war. The use of naval force in war does not count as gunboat diplomacy unless the victim is an ally or, in some cases, a neutral. If we compare the record of the 1970s with that of the 1920s, we may note a geographical change: Chinese rivers and Latin American coasts no longer set the principal scene. But the incidence of naval activity has not diminished and its importance has actually increased. The high point of the twenties – the intervention of 35 warships and 40 000 troops at Shanghai in 1927 – was certainly impressive, but it did not have the dangerous significance of the major international crisis that culminated in the Mediterranean confrontation of the US Sixth Fleet and the Soviet Fifth Eskadra in October 1973.

The 1980s – to be further considered in the next chapter – have maintained the character of gunboat diplomacy as an essentially twentieth-century activity. It may nevertheless be useful to consider, through a comparative analysis of selected examples, how far the principles governing the use or threat of limited naval force have changed since the end of the Second World War. The argument could, of course, begin much earlier, but the notion of historical continuity is one to which today's readers must be gently and gradually introduced.

SIMPLE AMPHIBIOUS OPERATION

In 1952 there occurred an incident which offers a suitable starting-point. Its colonialist flavour provides the appropriate link with the past. The *leitmotif* of oil is central to the preoccupations not only of the fifties, but of later decades. And it features a unit which then had only a military reputation: the Special Air Service Regiment – the SAS.

The setting was an island too small to appear in the average atlas: Pulau Sambu. Although situated only three miles beyond the port limits of Singapore (then a British colony), Pulau Sambu was legally part of Indonesia and, in practice, run by Shell. That huge multinational corporation owned the innumerable oil tanks that dominated the low-lying, featureless terrain and held 70 000 tons of motor spirit and 170 000 tons of fuel oil. One Shell subsidiary, the Anglo-Saxon Petroleum Company, operated the ships that filled and emptied these tanks. Another, the Shell Company of Singapore, was responsible for the operation of what was essentially a regional centre for wholesale distribution. The managerial staff on the island came from a third subsidiary, the Bataafsche Petroleum Maatschappij, whose oil fields in Indonesia were the source of most of the fuel in the tanks. Working under their direction on Pulau Sambu were several hundred Indonesian labourers with Eurasian or Chinese foremen and 50 or 60 of these foremen were British subjects.

One of them had made himself sufficiently unpopular with the workforce to be blamed for provoking a riot on 23 January 1952. He was injured and evacuated to hospital in Singapore, where his case acquired both legal and political importance. For Mr Kleinman, his name notwithstanding, was as British as Don Pacifico a century earlier and his sufferings prompted as Palmerstonian a response as the decayed state of the nation then permitted.

The British nation was impressively represented in Singapore. Beside the Governor, who ran the colony itself, there was the United Kingdom Commissioner-General for South East Asia, a kind of regional viceroy with ill-defined powers but wide responsibilities. There were also the three British Commanders-in-Chief for the Far East. They and their staffs, together with other agencies, were grouped in the British Defence Coordination Committee (Far East) under the chairmanship, whenever he was in Singapore and not touring South East Asia, of the Commissioner-General. This was the body that undertook the redress of Mr Kleinman's grievances and the protection of oil supplies for Malaya and South East Asia.

The first step was a telegram, on 26 January, to the British Chargé d'Affaires at Djakarta, asking him to tell the Indonesian Government of the riot, to point out that the five policemen available on the island were not enough to restore order, and to request the despatch of Indonesian naval patrol vessels to Pulau Sambu. Simultaneously, though this precaution was not disclosed to the British Chargé d'Affaires, HMS MORECAMBE BAY, a 1500–ton British frigate completed in 1949, was ordered to start patrolling off Pulau Sambu. Her 'action landing party' was mustered and exercised.

Indonesian cooperation was duly promised, but did not materialise soon enough to appease the mounting impatience in Singapore. On 1 February MORECAMBE BAY embarked five officers and 65 other ranks of the SAS Regiment before resuming her patrol off Pulau Sambu. The British Chargé d'Affaires at Djakarta, Charles Stewart, was told to warn the Indonesian Government that, unless Indonesian reinforcements reached Pulau Sambu on 2 February, British forces would land and restore order. The repetition of this telegram to the Foreign Office in London gave the British Government their intimation that an armed intervention in a foreign country was not merely intended, but imminent.

The news produced consternation in Whitehall and an attempt – frustrated by the time difference of seven-and-a-half hours – to countermand the ultimatum to the Indonesian Government. When the telegrams were eventually seen – many hours later – by Churchill, then Prime Minister, he produced the compromise instructions quoted at the beginning of this chapter: not soldiers, but armed police.

By the time his orders reached Singapore, someone on the British Defence Coordination Committee must have recalled, rather belatedly, the only epigram in the old Manual of Infantry Training: 'time spent on reconnaissance is seldom wasted.' Although launches carrying a police force of 75 Gurkhas and Malays with eight British officers did arrive off the island on the afternoon of 2 February, only a small reconnaissance party was sent ashore. They found the situation calm and the Shell representatives ashore no longer desirous of assistance. They re-embarked, no further landing took place, the night was uneventful and the next day, 3 February, saw the arrival of three Indonesian armed naval launches with a total of about 50 men aboard. But for the exchange of recriminations, the episode was over.[7]

This ill-managed and ultimately trivial affair symbolises the uneasy transition of even the simplest forms of gunboat diplomacy from a local initiative within the discretion of consuls and captains to an act of state exercised on the authority of a president or prime minister. It is significant that the official mainly responsible, in the temporary absence of his seniors, for diplomatic advice to the British Defence Coordination Committee in Singapore was G. V. Kitson, who had been a Consul in China from 1924 to 1942. Those years must have accustomed him to seeking naval assistance as soon as British subjects were endangered.

In the 1950s other instances of naval assistance to compatriots in danger on a foreign shore were on a larger scale. In 1951, for example, the cruiser HMS MAURITIUS was sent to Abadan for the protection and, ultimately, the evacuation of British subjects at the oil-refinery then operated by the Anglo-Iranian Oil Company. She was supported by the destroyers ARMADA, GRAVELINES, VIGO, CHEQUERS, CHIEFTAIN and CHIVALROUS. Although it was duly authorised by the British Government of the day, an adverse combination of political factors made this a controversial operation and it was cited by the Foreign Office as an unfortunate precedent when arguing that intervention at Pulau Sambu should be cancelled.

Nevertheless, when major riots occurred in Cairo at the end of January 1952 – almost simultaneously with the Pulau Sambu affair – a substantial British naval force was despatched from Malta to the coast of Egypt. The ships that were ready, but did not actually have to intervene, included the carrier OCEAN, the cruisers EURALYUS and GLASGOW, the destroyers CHIVALROUS, SAINTES, ARMADA, AISNE, JUTLAND, AGINCOURT and CORUNNA, together with the fast minelayer MANXMAN.[8] In 1955 the US Seventh Fleet organised evacuations from the Chinese Tachen Islands and from the mainland of North Vietnam. In 1956 the US Sixth Fleet landed marines at Alexandria and other Middle Eastern ports to protect more evacuations. All these were operations authorised by governments and executed by substantial forces.

The protection or the evacuation of their nationals in turbulent foreign parts intermittently preoccupied the naval powers during the 1960s and 1970s as well. Sometimes only precautions were involved. In 1967, in the angry aftermath of the Six Day War, no British

Embassy in the Middle East actually had to call for naval help to rescue endangered British subjects, but it was available. So it was (in this case HMS ALBION with 41 Commando Royal Marines) when, almost simultaneously, civil war began in Nigeria. In 1974 the commando carrier HERMES and HM Ships ANDROMEDA, BRIGHTON, DEVONSHIRE, HAMPSHIRE, ONSLAUGHT and RHYL evacuated some 1500 British and other refugees from Kyrenia beach in Cyprus after the Turkish invasion. Eighteen French warships were deployed off Djibouti in case they were needed by French citizens in 1977. Occasionally, as with the American intervention of 1965 in the Dominican Republic, reassuring expatriates seemed more of a pretext than a reason. But, in almost every case, these were deliberate operations executed by significant naval forces.

Perhaps the truest echo of the elegance and economy of force that was once the keynote of gunboat diplomacy came as late as 1986. In January of that year the Royal Yacht BRITANNIA, assisted by the survey ship HMS HYDRA and the merchant vessel DIAMOND PRINCESS, evacuated from Aden, then torn by civil war, 1379 people of 55 different nationalities and one French dog. BRITANNIA (who was on passage at the time) and her consorts were employed because, being unarmed, they could enter the territorial waters of the Peoples' Democratic Republic of Yemen without exciting opposition. This represented a sea-change – both in political attitudes and the means available for coastal defence – in the fifty years since the Spanish Civil War, when warships of various navies were repeatedly active round the coasts and in and out of the ports of Spain. Even in January 1986, however, the destroyer HMS NEWCASTLE and the frigate HMS JUPITER provided armed support outside territorial waters.[9]

The part played by the Royal Yacht was not the only unusual feature of this operation. No force had to be threatened or employed. Nobody seems to have objected. BRITANNIA even had a Russian officer on board, who provided liaison with Soviet ships evacuating their own citizens.[10] It was a reversion, probably fated to remain an exceptional reversion, to the old idea that navies could sometimes have an internationally acceptable, a humanitarian role in rescuing people endangered by a foreign conflict that did not concern them.

In the last forty years the naval powers have often found it more difficult to conduct inshore operations in foreign waters without arousing the active resentment of the coastal states concerned. Even humanitarian motives are not always accepted as justifying an unsolicited intervention. Many of these coastal states have also acquired, often quite cheaply, weapons with which to express their displeasure. In this new and more hostile environment the naval powers have naturally become more cautious. Decisions to intervene are reached at a higher level, after more anxious consideration and with less frequency than in an earlier era. A single warship is seldom considered sufficient as the modern equivalent of the traditional gunboat or cruiser. Naturally no other navy could hope to emulate the deployment of five aircraft carriers to evacuate American citizens from Saigon in 1975, but future planners may consider that a safer ideal at which to aim.

THE SUPERIOR SHIP OPERATION

No fallacy is harder to eradicate than the common notion that the major naval powers enjoy monopoly rights in gunboat diplomacy. Naturally a large navy has a greater capacity for the use or threat of limited force than a small navy. How far either exploits that capacity is a matter for political choice. For thirty-five years the Soviet Navy has been the world's second largest and second strongest – even ranking first when American admirals are asking Congress for money – but the Russian record in gunboat diplomacy compares poorly with that of lesser powers. The US Navy is normally a high scorer, but the intense activity of the Reagan era followed a season of something approaching unemployment under Carter. Both Super Powers, indeed all the principal naval powers, have themselves sometimes been the *victims* of gunboat diplomacy, which was employed during the 1970s by 23 different governments.[11]

This is particularly understandable when the target of attack is an isolated ship at sea. On 2 June 1967, for instance, the USS LIBERTY was deployed from the American naval base at Rota in Spain to the Eastern Mediterranean. LIBERTY was an electronic intelligence gatherer with four machine-guns as her only armament. Her mission was to monitor the radio communications of both sides in the Arab–Israeli War that began on 5 June, the day that LIBERTY reached her allotted position off Gaza. At 14.03 on 8 June she was some 14 miles out to sea, comfortably outside anybody's territorial waters, when the ship was attacked, first by Israeli aircraft, then by Israeli motor torpedo boats. LIBERTY was not sunk, but she was badly damaged, with most of her delicate equipment out of action, 34 of her crew dead and 171 wounded.

The Israeli Government promptly admitted the attack, claimed the LIBERTY had been mistaken for an Egyptian supply ship, and apologised. Many, but not all, subsequent commentators have tended to agree with Admiral Isaac Kidd, who presided over the US Naval Court of Inquiry held immediately afterwards, when he declared:

> The United States Navy wished to go on record as stating that while it had to accept the apologies of the Israeli Government it did not accept the explanation for the attack.[12]

Admiral Thomas H. Moorer, once he had retired from his post as Chairman of the Joint Chiefs of Staff, agreed with this verdict:

> I cannot accept the claim by the Israelis that this was a case of mistaken identity.[13]

LIBERTY was, after all, rather a recognisable ship with her extra radio-mast, numerous aerials and large sonar detectors. The Israelis also had quite enough expertise in the field of electronic intelligence to know what and where LIBERTY was before they ever saw her.

No thread, of course, is more conspicuous in the rich tapestry of naval history than the frequency with which ships at sea are wrongly identified, particularly by aircraft. On 16 June 1968, for instance, the USS BOSTON and HMAS HOBART were attacked and damaged by American aircraft in the Gulf of Tonkin.[14] Even in the clear visibility of a summer's day in the Mediterranean a mistake would have been conceivable. Two factors cast doubt on this explanation. The first was that Israeli aircraft made six separate inspections of LIBERTY on 8 June *before* the attack began.[15] The second was, as Anthony Pearson explains in his book,[16] that the Israelis protested too much, do not appear to have paid the compensation they promised and were not seriously pressed by unnaturally acquiescent and reticent Americans.

What the dog did not do in the night was particularly apparent, as Sherlock Holmes would have pointed out, after Richard K. Smith published his article (arguing that the attack on LIBERTY had been deliberate) in *United States Naval Institute Proceedings* for June 1978.[17] In spite of some stylistic eccentricities this is a journal of the highest standards, but neither its readers nor its writers are conspicuously neutral in their attitudes to the US Navy. Nevertheless twelve months elapsed before any of the numerous comments the journal published on this article endorsed its condemnation of the Israeli attack. Some remarkable influence must have been exerted to obscure the obvious.

Presuming the attack to have been deliberate need not commit us to acceptance of Pearson's elaborate conspiracy theories. Fighting men under strain can do outrageous things to neutrals – as those unfortunate British fishermen on the Dogger Bank discovered in 1904, when Russia's Second Pacific Squadron decided their trawlers were Japanese torpedo boats and blew them out of the water. The Israelis may have had important secrets to conceal from LIBERTY's eavesdroppers, but they may just have lost their temper. Their motives do not greatly matter. What is interesting is that a small country with little naval strength, a client state totally dependent for survival on the goodwill of the patron, could get away with such an insolent, such an altogether outrageous use of gunboat diplomacy 'to bite the hand that fed them'.

We are unlikely ever to learn how closely the lessons of the LIBERTY were studied in North Korea. They certainly received insufficient attention in Washington. Admiral Horacio Rivero, Jr, the Vice-Chief of Naval Operations, did decide that similar ships should in future carry 'at least 20-mm guns',[18] but the USS PUEBLO had only two machine guns when she was boarded and captured by North Korean patrol craft on 23 January 1968. It is perhaps surprising that sensitive missions in dangerous waters should have been given to ships as virtually defenceless as LIBERTY and PUEBLO. The USS MADDOX had been attacked by North Vietnamese torpedo boats while carrying out similar tasks in the Gulf of Tonkin on 2 August 1964. As a destroyer, MADDOX was able to beat off the attacks without herself sustaining any damage. A possible explanation may be found in one of the answers given by Robert S. McNamara, then US Secretary for Defense, to the Senate Foreign Relations Committee in 1968:

I haven't compared, myself, item by item, the equipment in the PUEBLO and the MADDOX, but I am told the MADDOX had much less sophisticated equipment and less of it, and was less capable, therefore, of electronic surveillance.[19]

The controversy surrounding the LIBERTY and the MADDOX is wholly absent in the case of the PUEBLO. Nobody, least of all the North Koreans, ever suggested that their exertion of limited naval force was accidental or resulted from any kind of mistake. It was almost certainly a deliberate operation intended to produce the result it actually achieved: putting an end to this particular form of American espionage against North Korea.[20]

It is still too early to be sure whether the attack of 17 May 1987 on the USS STARK was, as the Iraquis subsequently claimed, due to pilot error. If it was not, then this incident again emphasises that coastal states with few naval resources are not always helpless victims. Even the strongest naval powers sometimes find gunboat diplomacy an expensive game to play. Naturally it can be argued – as committees conducting post-mortems often do – that more cautious tactics would reduce the risks that cannot always be entirely eliminated. These may include loss of face as well as loss of life. The stranding of a *Whisky* class submarine near the Swedish naval base at Karlskrona in October 1981 was one of the rare instances in which that fate befell the usually cautious Soviet Navy.

Of course, the Super Powers were not alone in occasionally reminding the detached observer of Lord Salisbury's complaint at the end of the last century against

> that phase of British temper which in the last few months has led detachment after detachment of British troops into the most obvious ambuscades – mere arrogance.[21]

It was surely a little rash of the British Government of the day to send, unescorted, an unarmed ship bearing the provocative name of SHACKLETON into waters where, as the Chief of the Argentine Naval Staff had warned the British Naval Attaché in Buenos Aires, she would be arrested. Fortunately, in February 1976, Admiral Massera, the Commander-in-Chief, though willing to wound, was still afraid to strike and the Argentine destroyer that fired on SHACKLETON did not press home her attack.[22]

Of all these incidents only the attack provoked on 2 August 1964 by the mission MADDOX was conducting in the Gulf of Tonkin proved to be of lasting significance. That furnished part of the pretext for the most disastrous war yet conducted by the United States. The remainder were momentary crises; some briefly alarming; all distressing, sometimes fatal, to those involved; in retrospect, only blips on the oscilloscope of history.

They might have been more. In 1967 President Johnson had to countermand the order issued by the US Joint Chiefs of Staff after the attack on LIBERTY for the carriers AMERICA and SARATOGA to launch an air strike against the Israeli naval base at Haifa.[23] In 1968, in impotent anger at the seizure of PUEBLO and the taking hostage of her crew, the United States deployed a task-force in the Sea of Japan that included three carriers.[24] The use of limited naval force is seldom devoid of risk, but, if it leads to war, it forfeits any claim to the title of gunboat diplomacy.

OPPOSED AMPHIBIOUS OPERATION

That great chain of tropical islands, the Antilles, begins with Cuba, the largest and most westerly. It dwindles eastward some 1500 miles to little Antigua, then curves south to Grenada, gatepost of the Tobago Channel that joins the Caribbean Sea to the Atlantic Ocean. Grenada is a larger island (133 square miles) than Pulau Sambu. It can be found, even if only as a named dot, in the atlas. In 1983 its population – variously estimated around the 100 000 mark – greatly exceeded that of Pulau Sambu. There was neither oil, nor an oil company, nor, indeed, industry of any significance, but the island's farmers raised a variety of crops. Unfortunately these were insufficiently profitable. Even the hardy handful of foreign tourists prepared to overcome the sheer difficulty of getting to Grenada brought in a third as much as all her exports.

In 1979 it was not unreasonable of the Government of Grenada to suppose that building an airport at Point Salines able to handle large airliners would be the quickest way of boosting Grenada's earnings. Unfortunately the People's Revolutionary Government which seized power that year from an eccentric dictator (who had himself believed in the airport as well as in Unidentified Flying Objects) was indisputably Communist. Although orders for the construction and equipment of the airport were placed with companies in the United States and Europe (including the British Plessey), little finance was available from any source amenable to American influence. Most of the money (and many of the construction workers) came from Cuba, with whose international attitudes Grenada's rulers aligned themselves ever more closely.

It would be pointless to debate whether or not American hostility to Grenada's rulers was rationally or morally justified. Politically it was inevitable, as it had been in the case of Cuba twenty years earlier. Dubious arguments about the potential military value of the airport or the safety of United States citizens in Grenada or the appeal from Sir Paul Scoon, the Governor-General (which may even have been made after the invasion, while he was a guest on board the USS GUAM, and given an earlier date) only confused the issue.[25] Even under President Carter a harder line had begun to emerge in the Caribbean in May 1980, when Operation Solid Shield involved 42 warships and the landing of 2000 marines at the surviving American enclave in Cuba at Guantanamo Bay.[26]

Soon after Reagan had succeeded Carter, the US Navy had made an even more relevant demonstration. Notionally part of a larger NATO exercise Ocean Venture 81, Operation Amber took place in August 1981 on the island of Vieques close to Puerto Rico.

The scenario for the exercise was that the government of the island of Amber and the Amberines, which was hostile to the US, had seized US citizens as hostages. US forces were to invade the island, rescue the hostages and then 'instal a regime favorable to the way of life we espouse.'

It was scarcely surprising that Maurice Bishop, Prime Minister of Grenada, concluded that Rear-Admiral Robert McKenzie had really meant Grenada and the Grenadines when he talked of 'Amber and the Amberines'. There was actually a place called Amber close to the new international airport at Point Salines. Bishop's protests were brushed aside by Al Haig, then US Secretary of State.[27]

On 25 March 1983 President Reagan appeared on television (mainly to talk about the Strategic Defense Initiative) and argued that Cuban assistance in building the airport at Point Salines was a threat to the national security of the United States. American naval manoeuvres six miles off the coast of Grenada gave his views an extra edge.[28]

No politically advantageous opportunity for intervention presented itself before the autumn of that year. Then, in October 1983, a suicidal feud erupted within the Central Committee of Grenada's ruling party. Maurice Bishop, who was party leader as well as Prime Minister, was arrested on 12 October and, on 19 October, he and some 60 others were murdered. Fidel Castro was particularly shocked. The Cuban newspaper *Granma* published his condemnation the following day:

> No doctrine, no principle calling itself revolutionary and no internal split can justify such atrocious acts as the physical elimination of Bishop and the prominent group of honest and dignified leaders who died yesterday.[29]

Perhaps nobody in Washington actually commented that, when rogues fall out, honest men come by their own, but it was on 21 October that two American naval groups on their way to the Eastern Mediterranean were diverted towards Grenada. The first was

Mediterranean Amphibious Ready Group 1–84, comprising the amphibious assault ship GUAM (Commodore Erie), four other amphibious ships and 2000 marines. The second, steaming 150 miles north of the amphibious group, was a carrier battle-group centred on INDEPENDENCE and commanded by Rear-Admiral Berry. Orders for an assault landing on Grenada were issued during the night of 23 October, Vice-Admiral Metcalf arrived by helicopter to take command of both groups on 24 October, and the main landing began in the early hours of 25 October 1983.[30]

Not only marines were involved. Rangers of the US Army parachuted in to seize the airfield at Point Salines and were followed by airportable elements of the 82nd Airborne Division. Altogether the landing force numbered about 6000 and included a variety of armoured vehicles. By 31 October the strength of US military personnel on Grenada had reached its peak of 7335. An extra 300 soldiers from Commonwealth Caribbean countries (mainly Barbados and Jamaica) arrived on 28 October, after most of the fighting was over, to give the operation a slightly less American image and to undertake some policing duties.[31]

Because of the reticence still observed by the United States Government and the initial exclusion of the media (fifteen reporters were given a day trip to Grenada on 27 October) it is hard to be sure how much opposition the American had to overcome. An official statement on 7 November said that some 1800 members of the People's Revolutionary Army and the militia had surrendered and a further 750 were thought to be at large. How many had taken any part in the fighting is uncertain, but the Americans only claimed to have killed 45.[32] Other accounts speak of Grenadian soldiers throwing away their arms and fleeing as soon as the Americans landed. Five weeks before the invasion the Central Committee of the New Jewel Movement (as the Grenadian Communists called themselves) had reached the censorious conclusion that the militia was non-existent and the army demoralised.[33] Cuban construction workers (some 700 strong) were armed and fought when attacked, but there were few, if any, heavy or sophisticated weapons on Grenada.

American writers have criticised many aspects of Operation Urgent Fury, including the number of helicopters lost and the ratio of American casualties attributable to accident or 'friendly fire'. Nevertheless, the fighting was over by the beginning of November; the last foreign Communists (including some rather roughly-treated diplomats) left on 4 November; and on 9 November Sir Paul Scoon,

the Governor-General who had survived both the 1979 coup d'état
and the crisis of October 1983 to remain Grenada's constitutional
Head of State, was able to nominate a new interim government until
such time as an election could be held. This took place on 5 December
1984 and was won by Herbert Blaize, an elderly but acceptable politician from Grenada's colonial past. The controversial airport at Point
Salines had opened a little earlier, having been completed with funds
provided by the United States and other respectable donors. There
remained on the island only 250 American soldiers.[34]

The United States had achieved their purpose – the eradication of
a Communist regime in the Caribbean – swiftly and at the cost of
only 19 Americans killed and 108 wounded – less than the casualties
aboard LIBERTY in 1967.[35] Naturally the forces employed were very
large and their superiority over the enemy even greater. The 7335
men the United States landed in Grenada, for instance, may be
compared with the 10 000 Britain landed in the Falklands to fight an
outright war against a fully-equipped Argentine garrison of whom
12 978 were taken prisoner.[36] At sea and in the air the Americans
were unopposed, but 100 helicopters and the 70 combat aircraft
aboard INDEPENDENCE provided far more air support than the British
had ever enjoyed in the Falklands. The launching of 700 aircraft
sorties from INDEPENDENCE in less than a week also suggests fewer
restrictions on their use[37] and civilian casualties on Grenada were
tenfold greater than in the whole of the Falklands War.

American achievements in gunboat diplomacy notwithstanding,
the US Navy have always had reservations about the idea of *limited*
naval force. They prefer an ample margin of strength and the use of
as much force as may be required. The first preference is one most
navies would share, if only they could afford it, and the case for
restricting the application of force is political rather than naval or
even, as is sometimes argued, legal. It is usually – not always –
advantageous for an assailant to be perceived as using less force,
particularly less violence, than the resources he has deployed would
permit. This perception gives the victim an incentive to yield – and
his allies, actual or potential, a motive for abstention – for fear of
worse. Needless violence, on the other hand, may prompt a desperate
resort to escalation. In the case of Grenada – and the balance of
argument always depends on particular circumstances – it is conceivable that a more circumspect approach might have allowed the
Americans to achieve their objective with fewer casualties. The
evidence available, however, is insufficient to answer such questions

as: was it really necessary to attack the Cuban airport-builders?

These were not, as it happens, the issues which most exercised foreign governments. In the United Nations and elsewhere the Americans were criticised for intervening at all rather than for their conduct of the actual operation. Except for those small Caribbean states which made token contributions to Urgent Fury, only Chile, El Salvador and Israel expressed support for the United States, who had to use their veto to escape condemnation by the Security Council. Even Mrs Thatcher, usually President Reagan's most faithful disciple, had to equivocate and the Russians greatly enjoyed the chance to censure the United States in the very words the Americans had applied in 1979 to Soviet action in Afghanistan.[38]

For these adverse reactions the Government of the United States must accept much of the blame. Urgent Fury, though obviously contemplated for years, had been sloppily prepared. The marines had no proper maps and the soldiers did not know the location of the American citizens they were supposed to be rescuing (who had themselves not been told that they were in danger).[39] Intelligence about the state of the defences was both inadequate and inaccurate. The political basis for the operation was improvised at the last moment and not surprisingly proved to be implausible and even internally inconsistent. Worst of all, the allies of the United States received neither prior warning nor even a prompt explanation of the accomplished fact. All this formed a deplorable contrast with President Kennedy's handling of the Cuban Missile Crisis in 1962: the special envoys to allied capitals (even Charles de Gaulle was convinced) and the immediate despatch of aerial photographs to US embassies throughout the world (President Sukarno of Indonesia had a set 36 hours after Kennedy's speech).

Against insignificant opposition Urgent Fury achieved its objectives and the United States easily survived the international criticism they had needlessly excited. The operation is likely, however, to be studied in staff colleges less as model than as an instructive example of muddling through – rich in mistakes to be avoided. In war, secrecy and surprise may be overriding considerations. In violent peace the political consequences of applying limited naval force also need prior consideration.

This is actually more important today than it used to be. The climate of international opinion has altered, as has the naval environment, to the disadvantage of gunboat diplomacy. In 1927, when 35 warships and 40 000 troops and marines were deployed at Shanghai, these forces had been supplied by eight different nations, including all the Great Powers of the day: Britain, France, Italy, Japan and the United States. China was merely the victim: paralysed by her own anarchy. Germany and the Soviet Union, for different reasons, had withdrawn from the international scene. There was nobody that mattered left to protest.

Ten years later, at the end of January 1937, civil war in Spain was six months old and the British navy had carried 17 000 Spaniards to safety from many different ports in Spain. British warships had also, as had those of France, Germany, Italy and the United States, rescued their own nationals and those of third countries. The five governments differed sharply in their attitudes towards the Spanish Civil War, but managed to tolerate the naval presence of their rivals, whose sailors would exchange courtesies, scraps of information, even some kinds of help.

In July 1936 a British diplomat swam out to a French warship anchored off San Sebastián with messages (which the ship obligingly transmitted) from both his own ambassador and the German Chargé d'Affaires appealing to their respective governments for naval assistance in evacuation.

The warring Spaniards sometimes objected to interference by foreign warships around their coasts, but even Spaniards usually acquiesced, occasionally expressed appreciation, when endangered Spanish women and children were rescued. Japan was too distant to care, but the Soviet Union (once again internationally active but not yet a significant naval power) actually chartered the British ss BRAMSDEN and sought British naval protection (which was granted) for the evacuation of Spanish children from Gijón in September 1937.[40]

Before 1939 there existed no consensus of international opinion ready to condemn any naval intervention merely because this entailed the infringement of national sovereignty. The naval powers were particularly chary of censuring in others a course of action they might themselves have reason to imitate. Naturally this was no more than a presumption of innocence which could be, and often was, overturned by political considerations or the particular circumstances of the case. The shifting, over the years, of the burden of proof has nevertheless been remarkable. In 1923 the Council of the League of Nations managed to condone the bombardment and seizure of the island of Corfu by the Italian Navy as a means of extorting from the government of Greece compensation for the murder of General Enrico Tellini.

In the 1930s the Japanese Navy attracted Anglo-American criticism for conduct in China comparable to earlier performances by the navies of Britain and the United States.

After 1945 the United Nations, initially willing to concede a degree of privilege in intervention, a kind of *droit de seigneur*, first to the United States, then to other powers (India in the case of Goa, for instance), moved steadily towards a consensus on the illegitimacy of any forcible challenge to national sovereignty. In April 1982 the Security Council condemned the Argentine invasion of the Falkland Islands by 10 votes to 1 and 4 abstentions. Yet, on almost every other occasion, before and since, a large majority of the United Nations have wanted Britain to enter into negotiations with Argentina over sovereignty in the Falklands. It was only the Argentine resort to force that stuck in the international craw.

In October 1983 better political preparation and more skilful diplomacy were certainly needed, but might not have been enough to win international acceptance for Operation Urgent Fury. What is more significant is that international opposition neither deterred the United States nor detracted from the success of this recent example of the most ambitious kind of gunboat diplomacy: the opposed amphibious operation. Urgent Fury can reasonably be compared with the French amphibious operation against Bizerta in 1961, though the American landing of 1965 in the Dominican Republic was on a larger scale and the resulting occupation lasted longer. So did the Turkish seizure of Eastern Cyprus in Operation Attila of July 1974. That also involved heavier fighting. Not much is known about the Chinese descent of the same year on the Paracel Islands or the Indonesian, in December 1975, on East Timor, but the forces engaged would have been smaller.

Urgent Fury thus takes its place in a continuing tradition of the political application, by many governments and in various parts of the world, of limited naval force. It was not the largest operation of the kind and by no means the bloodiest, just the most recent. If it was internationally contentious, American intervention seems to have been welcomed by many in Grenada. In the United States it was popular. The US Army alone distributed 10 000 decorations.[41]

Unkind critics have also argued the Urgent Fury was conducted with an incompetence that could have been disastrous against a serious enemy. An obsession with secrecy left many American participants as uncertain of their own objectives as they were ignorant of the role of other units. Confusion was compounded by the use of so many special and semi-secret forces – the Night Stalkers, the Sea Air Land Team, Delta Force – as well as various formations of the Air Force, the Army, the Marines and the Navy. The persistent failure of communications was matched by the paucity of intelligence and the neglect of prior reconnaissance. There were thus military as well as political lessons to be learned.[42]

Although recent decades have seen the growth of obstacles – political, naval and technological – even this most difficult kind of gunboat diplomacy has survived. Lesser varieties, which will be further explored in the next chapter, have almost flourished. Of course much has changed. No aspect of diplomacy, politics or war is entirely unaltered. We live in a world that is always different, but in which many strands of continuity may be perceived on careful inspection. The principles of gunboat diplomacy are certainly not the most important of these persistent factors, but they somehow contrive to linger on.

5 Gunboat Diplomacy in the 1980s and Beyond

> The US Navy has always been used by Washington as a major instrument of the policy of expansion it pursues in the world. – BARSEGOV[1]

> Freedom to use the seas is our nation's lifeblood. For that reason, our Navy is designed to keep the sealanes open world-wide. – REAGAN[2]

In earlier chapters various incidents were mentioned in which the use of limited naval force had a swift and obvious result. Barely four weeks were needed to demonstrate the failure of the Argentine Operation Rosario in 1982 (gunboat diplomacy is always accounted a failure if it leads to war); ten days to establish the success of Operation Urgent Fury against Grenada; less than 24 hours to register American acquiescence in Israeli action against the LIBERTY in 1967.

Such prompt and conclusive verdicts are rare in the history of gunboat diplomacy. During the 1920s and 1930s, for instance, encounters in Chinese waters, particularly in Chinese rivers, were very numerous. It was often possible to argue that a given naval intervention had either prevailed or been rebuffed in its immediate purpose. Until 1949, however, both the Chinese and the naval powers had demonstrably failed to achieve their long-term aims. China was never free from foreign interference in her internal affairs, and foreigners in China could not count on a degree of Chinese tolerance and protection acceptable to their own governments. Low-level conflict could have continued indefinitely, if it had not happened that major political change gave China a government able and determined to maintain the country's sovereign independence.

1945, so often regarded as the century's great historical watershed, has not eliminated the protracted struggle. Israel has known little peace and Indochina even less. Both have occasionally attracted the attentions of foreign navies. The Mediterranean, the Caribbean, the Persian Gulf have emerged, sometimes in different years, as the modern heirs of the old China Station. Even in other seas various governments have occasionally threatened or employed limited naval force. The results, whether considered good or bad, were seldom so decisive as to persuade all concerned that no further action need ever be contemplated.

Continuing disputes, intermittently sharpening towards conflict, whether or not this involves actual violence, often feature in relations between states. Not a year, scarcely even a month or a week, has passed since 1945 without friction between the United States and the Soviet Union. It is hard to imagine how or when the relationship between the Super Powers might become as much a matter of workaday routine as that between Britain and Brazil. The chronic hostility of the Super Powers is not unique. India and Pakistan, Greece and Turkey, North and South Korea are lesser pairs of durable antagonists. Very various methods of bringing these disputes to a conclusion, even to some compromise not wholly ephemeral, have been tried and have failed. It was regrettable that Britain's fishery dispute with Iceland should have lasted, off and on, for nearly twenty years, but the duration was less remarkable than the ability of both sides to keep their use of naval force limited.

Ideally, it might be argued, governments would do better simply to endure those ills for which they cannot reasonably expect to find an early cure. If the injury is serious, however, it is hard for any government to admit that there is no remedy they can usefully attempt. The difficulty increases with the pretensions of the government concerned. Moreover, the political disadvantages of admitting impotence are immediate and certain. The risk that endeavour might fail is more hypothetical and a little distant, thus less daunting. And few politicians realise – not Eisenhower in 1954, nor Brezhnev in 1979 – how much easier is involvement, whether in Vietnam or in Afghanistan, than eventual disengagement. It is not surprising that so many governments bite off more than they can chew.

OUTSIDE NAVIES IN THE GULF

The Iraqui Government did that when they attacked Iran in September 1980. When they later realised their mistake and tried, more than once, to start negotiations, they failed again. If any of the distant governments who sent warships to the Gulf – notably, but not exclusively, those of Britain, France, the Soviet Union and the United States – have had similar doubts, they have yet to admit any change of heart.

For most of the 1970s Iran was the dominant naval power in the

Persian Gulf. Britain ended in 1971 the protectorates she had long exercised over some of the coastal states and British warships became less frequent visitors. The two destroyers and an HQ vessel the US Navy usually based at Bahrain were not their most modern ships, nor was command of this Middle East Force a particularly coveted appointment. When the USS CONSTELLATION entered the Gulf on a 'familiarisation mission' in 1974, she was the first American carrier to do so for 23 years.

The Shah of Iran, however, profited by the high price of oil (which he had helped to boost) to enlarge and modernise his navy, buying ships from the United States and other members of NATO. He did so as part of his drive for national grandeur, but, by and large, Iranian naval dominance served American purposes as well.

When the power of the Shah crumbled in 1978 and he had to flee the country in January 1979, the US Navy sent extra destroyers to the Gulf. In February 1979 they evacuated American citizens and other foreigners from Iranian ports on the Gulf. In March CONSTELLATION was despatched to the Arabian Sea. At this stage the United States Government was still understandably uncertain of the nature of the problem it faced. Was there a local upheaval in Iran? Were the Russians behind it? Did it involve a threat to the oil supplies of the West?

Harold Brown, US Secretary of Defense, tried to cover all these contingencies by declaring:

> we will take any action that is appropriate to safeguard production of oil and its transportation to consumer nations without interference from hostile powers.[3]

But the partial loss of Iranian oil in 1979 and the general increase in oil prices turned out to be tolerable by consumers; due to internal disturbances in Iran, and not really amenable to naval intervention.

Nor did the American naval presence, outside the Gulf and in the Indian Ocean, do anything to reduce the increasingly anti-American attitudes of the Iranian revolutionaries. Nevertheless, in November 1979, when the US Embassy in Tehran was attacked and the staff taken hostage, the USS KITTY HAWK was ordered to join MIDWAY in the Indian Ocean. For the next two years there would seldom be less than two American carrier battle-groups in the Indian Ocean, occasionally even three.

This was an extreme case of the *catalytic* threat of limited naval force in a situation in which danger is probable but its nature uncertain.

> Something, it is felt, is going to happen, which might somehow be prevented if force were available at the critical point.[4]

So ships are deployed before any decision – which may, indeed, never be reached – is taken on how to use them. Moreover, in Washington confusion still prevailed. President Carter was obviously thinking of the Soviet Union when he proclaimed on 28 January 1980 that

> an attempt by any outside force to gain control of the Persian Gulf will be regarded as an assault on the vital interests of the USA.[5]

Soviet destroyers and frigates based at Socotra had started intermittent patrols in the Arabian Sea and the Straits of Hormuz in 1979. But they, and the intelligence trawlers that also made frequent appearances, seemed more concerned to keep an eye on the US Navy than to stir up the hornets' nest ashore. Although the total number of Soviet ships in the Indian Ocean rose to as many as thirty in April 1980 (afterwards gradually declining) there were seldom more than two major surface combatants at a time.[6]

April 1980 was also the month in which the United States tried and failed to rescue the Americans held hostage in their embassy at Tehran. Whether the attempt might have succeeded if an American carrier had entered the Gulf (covered by aircraft from another outside) and then launched helicopters on a much shorter flight is a question as controversial as it is hypothetical. The limited operation actually attempted under much less favourable conditions was a fiasco damaging to American prestige.

But it was war between Iran and Iraq that brought other navies to the Gulf. In October 1980 the Royal Navy diverted two ships from a Far Eastern cruise to the Gulf. They were later relieved (from home waters) to start the Armilla Patrol, which has been maintained ever since – usually two destroyers or frigates with supporting auxiliaries. The purpose declared by the British Ministry of Defence was 'protection of merchant shipping'.[7] A combined exercise, Beacon Compass, was held with the US Navy (which now had 22 warships in the Indian Ocean, including the carriers RANGER and EISENHOWER). By 15 October the arrival of French and Australian ships had brought the Western total to 60. The Soviet Union had 29.[8]

The 'threat to the free passage of merchant shipping'[9] in the Gulf was real enough. Although the major campaign, particularly against tankers, began only in 1984, the Iranian Navy seized a Danish ship carrying explosives to Iraq as early as August 1981. Iraqui aircraft attacked tankers in December 1982, and neutral shipping in the Gulf was considered at risk from May 1981 onwards. By the end of 1983 at least 23 merchant ships had been attacked. Insofar as such ships could be protected by foreign navies, a good case existed for their presence in the Gulf.

In practice, unfortunately, it did not work out that way. April 1984 is the generally accepted date for the beginning of the main Iraqui campaign against tankers exporting Iranian oil and earning Iran the money with which to buy munitions of war. Successful Iranian offensives against Iraqui ports at the head of the Gulf had put a stop to the seaborne export of Iraqui oil by the end of 1980. Iraq had to rely entirely on pipelines across land frontiers and, so far as oil exports were concerned, had nothing to lose by making the Gulf unsafe. In March 1985 it was reckoned that a total of 127 ships had been attacked, mostly by Iraq, but the figures estimated by different authors do vary.

Naturally it was not long before Iran retaliated. In the virtual absence of seaborne traffic to and from Iraqui ports, these attacks – mainly by Iranian aircraft – were directed against tankers and other ships trading with the Arab Gulf States that supported Iraq. In 1986 Iran made increasing use of naval vessels, including fast patrol craft bought from Sweden, both to stop and search merchant ships and to attack them. A conservative estimate of the total number of merchant ships attacked by the middle of 1987 is 200 – of which attacks about 125 were made by Iraqui forces. Most press reports quote higher figures. Over 100 sailors were killed and some 7 million tons of shipping were lost.

These are substantial casualties to be suffered in the presence of so many powerful navies originally sent to the Gulf 'to keep the sealanes open'. Sir Adrian Swire, Chairman of the International Chamber of Shipping, offers a partial explanation:

Taking a random six-month period – the first six months of 1986 – there were 24 recorded attacks on merchant vessels, of which nine involved Liberian flag ships, six Cypriot, five Maltese, two Iranian and one each from the Netherlands and the Federal Republic of Germany. This pattern is broadly typical for the whole three years since the attacks started. Not only do most vessels have no form of naval protection available to them in the Gulf, they also in many cases fly the flag of states with only limited international political influence. They are therefore vulnerable in every sense.[10]

The conclusion drawn by the International Chamber of Shipping was that an United Nations naval force was needed to deter such attacks. The difficulty of reaching the necessary measure of international agreement must have been obvious not only to the Chamber, but to others who supported the idea: unions representing officers and men of the merchant marine, for instance, or, during discussion in the House of Commons in October 1987, the British Labour Party. But there was also dissatisfaction with the results of mere naval 'presence', not only because these warships were concerned with so small a proportion of the merchant vessels using the Gulf, but because there were too few of them (particularly in the case of the Armilla Patrol) to be widely present or for most of the time.

These ideas early attracted some Soviet support. Before the end of 1987 these crystallised in an article, 'A Soviet solution to the Gulf Problem', written by Alexander Ivan Galtsin of the Soviet Foreign Ministry for *Jane's Defence Weekly* (28 November 1987):

> Obviously merchant vessels must be defended and the Soviet Union was the first to heed the request by Kuwait for convoying oil tankers . . . the normalisation of the situation in the Gulf cannot be the prerogative of one state or a group of states . . . the best immediate step would be establishing a UN peacekeeping naval force in the region, including, if necessary, the naval ships of both the USA and the Soviet Union.

Naturally Russian dedication to altruistic multilateralism should not be exaggerated. When the Soviet merchant ship PYOTR YEMTSOV carrying arms to Iraq was intercepted and detained for two days by Iran in September 1986, Soviet naval reinforcements were sent to the Gulf.[11] The Russian attitude to gunboat diplomacy may be a trifle bashful, but they have not entirely eschewed the practice.

For these and other reasons, the lesson of the years from 1980 to 1986 is not entirely clear-cut. If there were few attacks on ships flying the American, British, French and Russian flags, was this because these nations maintained warships in or near the Gulf, or simply because relatively few merchant ships in the Gulf flew these flags? On 28 October 1987, for instance, Ian Stewart, British Minister of State for the Armed Forces told the House of Commons that only six British merchant ships had been attacked in the Gulf since the

Armilla Patrol began in 1980. In response to subsequent enquiries the Ministry of Defence were kind enough to provide comparative estimates of total number of ships using the Gulf in that period: all flags 16 800; British 1680. This suggests that 1.25 per cent of all ships using the Gulf (if we accept the conservative figure of 200) were attacked, but only 0.5 per cent of ships flying the British flag.

Comparing estimates is guesswork, of course, but it may offer a modest advance on the merely anecdotal evidence. That sometimes implies that outside warships failed in their task. They did not prevent the Iranian Navy from stopping and searching British and American vessels in January 1986. When the opportune presence in the Gulf of Oman of the destroyer USS DAVID R. RAY deterred the Iranians from similar interference, this seemed to newspaper readers to be one of the relatively rare instances of conspicuous success for a remarkably expensive naval deployment.

In other countries it is often assumed that the resources of the US Navy are infinitely elastic, but the two years from November 1979 to October 1981, when two and sometimes three carrier battle-groups were deployed in the Indian Ocean, imposed a greater strain than any comparable period since the Korean War.[12] The Arabian Sea is about as far as a ship can get from either coast of the continental United States. Climatic conditions are particularly trying and there are no agreeable ports to offer sailors a welcome break from endless patrolling. Diego Garcia is a useful base devoid of other attractions. In 1980 the nuclear-powered carrier NIMITZ managed 100 days at sea in the Indian Ocean, but discipline suffered among her crew. In 1987 the American naval deployment was said to be costing an *extra* 1.7 million dollars a day.[13]

The other naval powers never attempted to match the magnitude of the American presence, but their efforts were not insignificant. In 1987 the British, French and Russians all increased their deployments, conspicuously so in the case of the French. After keeping a low profile for years – modest ships and few of them – the French sent the carrier CLEMENCEAU to the Gulf in August 1987. The USS CONSTELLATION – the real veteran of a theatre visited by most American carriers – was again in the Arabian Sea and the battleship MISSOURI on her way.

That summer also saw two developments which, if not entirely new, had hitherto been sufficiently infrequent to seem almost random occurrences. The first was that ships flying the flag of naval powers were attacked. The case of the USS STARK, damaged by an Exocet missile from an Iraqui aircraft, has already been mentioned. In May 1987 the Russian cargo ship IVAN KOROTEYEV was hit by rocket-fire from unidentified (presumably Iranian) patrol boats. In July Iranian gunboats attacked the French freighter VILLE D'ANVERS.[14]

The second development was the appearance of mines. Oddly enough this seemed to surprise the naval powers in 1987. Yet the Iranian Navy had threatened, as early as October 1980, to mine the Straits of Hormuz if other Arab governments gave Iraq military assistance. In December 1981 *United States Naval Institute Proceedings* published an article speculating how this might be done. When floating mines were found in June 1983, these were assumed to have broken away from a field laid by Iraq at the northern end of the Persian Gulf in 1981 or 1982.

The Russians, it seems, were able to deploy a few minesweepers soon after the tanker MARSHAL CHUIKOV (which had been leased to Kuwait) hit a mine in May 1987. The Americans, whose preoccupation with more glamorous naval construction had led them to neglect provision for mine warfare, found it harder to react swiftly when the tanker BRIDGETON struck a mine in July 1987 or when the tanker TEXACO CARIBBEAN did so on 10 August – the second ship, alarmingly, outside the Straits of Hormuz and thus beyond what had hitherto been considered the war zone. It was 16 August before the small carrier GUADALCANAL reached Bahrain with minehunting helicopters flown out from the United States.

This was nevertheless a faster response than their allies (initially handicapped by political reservations about the wisdom of any commitment in the Gulf) could manage. Early in September 1987, however, British, Dutch, French and Italian minesweepers were in the Gulf or on the way. A Belgian decision was expected, as was the eventual arrival of such vessels as the US Navy could muster. All these countries were members of the North Atlantic Alliance, but there was no initial disposition to place these ships under a single commander. French naval officers, of course, had always distanced themselves in the Gulf from their allies and the Netherlands now preferred an *ad hoc* arrangement whereby their minesweepers worked with the Belgians, and could, if necessary, call on the British ships of the Armilla Patrol for armed assistance.

No Western government echoed Soviet complaints that the American naval presence in the Gulf and the adjoining seas reflected hostility towards the Soviet Union rather than concern for the safety of seaborne trade, but the ambiguous stance of the United States

Government had aroused concern in European capitals, as, indeed, it had in Washington itself. Keeping carrier battle-groups on call in the vicinity, as the United States had done since 1979, was not the obvious way to prevent sporadic attacks by single aircraft or fast motor boats on merchant ships. Nor was this achieved. From 1984 onwards, admittedly, such US warships as actually entered the Gulf had manifested intermittent interest in the safety of tankers. Not being organised or systematic, the protection thus offered was not always welcome to would-be neutral tanker-masters.[15] Only in 1987, when a number of Kuwaiti tankers were re-registered under the American flag, were proper convoys run – for a few ships at a time.

Kuwait, incidentally, had earlier sought a measure of insurance against war-risks by chartering Russian freighters, and most of the Gulf States were reluctant to commit themselves by making shore facilities available to the United States or other naval powers. Ashore or afloat there were obvious reservations about the value of American naval protection and anxiety lest its political price might prove excessive.

Even countries depending on oil from the Persian Gulf – Japan, for instance – preferred to avoid involving themselves in the protection of tankers. European allies were not sorry that the Persian Gulf was outside the North Atlantic Treaty Area. Even the British naval presence, otherwise welcome to the United States, had been a little detached and non-committal. In May 1987 the Defence Committee of the House of Commons published the statement made to them of the official British attitude:

> HMG is aware of, and has itself made, no proposals for organised cooperation.[16]

In 1987 sending minesweepers, which even the Soviet Deputy Foreign Minister, Vladimir Petrovsky, had been willing to exempt from his renewed call for the withdrawal of all foreign warships,[17] was an unprovocative response to American anxiety for Western solidarity. But the gesture would have lost its blandness – indeed, its acceptability in European capitals – if these vessels had been placed under American command. Rafsanjani, the Speaker of the Iranian parliament, went even further, describing the American naval presence in the Gulf as 'a flame near a powder-keg'.[18]

October 1987 had already brought a new flare of violence to the Gulf, with Iranian attacks on two American-flagged tankers, and American retaliation against a disused oil platform serving as an occasional base for Iranian Revolutionary Guards, but did not greatly increase international cooperation. The Russians were predictably critical of the American response, as were the Chinese. The British were verbally supportive. The French Navy, who had escorted the French tanker CHAUMONT (previously attacked in March 1986) into the Gulf in October 1987, escorted her out again in November. Oddly, the correspondent of *The Times* was surprised when the Italian frigate GRECALE convoyed an Italian tanker, the AMBRONIA, laden with Iranian oil.[19] The Soviet Army newspaper *Krasnaya Zvezda*, on the other hand, rather went out of its way to report that a Soviet destroyer on escort duty in the Gulf had warned off an Iranian frigate, which was menacing a Russian tanker.[20] As the total of ships attacked reached 400,[21] optimistic observers wondered whether they were again witnessing belated naval conversions to the doctrine of convoy.

OUTLOOK UNSETTLED

The year 1987 reached its end, but war continued between Iran and Iraq. In the Gulf, ships were still attacked – the Singapore-registered tanker NORMAN ATLANTIC was actually sunk by Iranian gunboats in December.[22] Outside navies kept an eye on one another and on such merchant ships as flew the same flag. Ensigns, indeed, were proliferating. The Iranian Chargé d'Affaires in Canberra had to protest when the Australian Navy offered divers to assist American mine-clearing operations.[23] The Persian Gulf, it seemed, had become the latest successor to the Yangtse River as the principal theatre of that perennial drama: gunboat diplomacy.

Half a century and more ago the Yangtse gunboats saw more action, but today's warships – in the Gulf or the Arabian Sea or the Indian Ocean – excite more anxiety. What worries the international spectators is not what the naval powers are actually doing. Even attacks on tankers, sailors killed or injured, cargoes lost in whole or part: beyond the narrow confines of the seafaring community these wanton spurts of malice are seldom accorded as much as a paragraph in the press. *The Times*, a newspaper of record, devoted less than a hundred words to the loss of the NORMAN ATLANTIC.

The question that preoccupies the foreign ministries, the strategists, the admirals and the defence analysts is: what will happen when somebody *wins* the Gulf War? It was long generally supposed that, sooner or later, Iran would defeat Iraq. What then would become of those Gulf States that helped, however bashfully, to finance the Iraqui war effort? Kuwait, the United Arab Emirates, even Saudi Arabia, are rich but not populous. They have neither the manpower, nor the enthusiasm, nor the experience of war enjoyed by the Iranians. If Iraq crumbles, only the United States may be able to save the Arabs of the Gulf and their 40 odd per cent of world oil reserves from Holy War. Neither the present price, nor the oil glut, nor one or two allies of the United States might survive the loss of Gulf oil.

Naturally a wide range of scenarios is conceivable for the ending of hostilities. Iran might even be defeated, superior numbers and fervour notwithstanding. So far the Ayatollahs have been remarkably successful in maintaining military discipline and civilian morale in seven years of war that have brought Iran more death than glory, but they may not be able to keep it up for ever. In late 1988 it seemed that fighting might dwindle into the stalemate of mutual exhaustion. Or a combination of international pressure, arms embargos and recalcitrant creditors might coerce the belligerents into uneasy truce. It is the pessimists who fear the emergence of direct confrontation between the United States and Iranian fanatics – flushed with victory and covertly supported by the Soviet Union.

There is more than precedent – the switching of Soviet support in the 1970s from losing Somalis to their stronger enemies, the Ethiopians – on which to base a prediction that the Russians would abandon a defeated Iraq and woo a successful Iran. In Moscow it might seem that encouraging the Iranians to strike south-west into Saudi Arabia and the sheikdoms of the Gulf would usefully divert their attention away from Soviet Moslems across Iran's northern frontier and from equally Moslem Afghan guerrillas to the east. And the impact of further fighting on oil supplies to the United States and their allies could only be gratifying.

In spite of seven years of cautious prudence in Moscow, such dark conjectures of likely Soviet reactions to one possible outcome of the war between Iran and Iraq are not altogether implausible and they help to explain the constant presence in the Indian Ocean of more of the US Navy than could ever be employed in the protection of merchant shipping in the Gulf. From 1979 onwards the Americans have wanted to be ready – if not for the worst, at any rate for a good deal more than gunboat diplomacy.

In 1987 American policy remained as widely focused as it had been in 1979.

The intensification of the Iran–Iraq war currently threatens [our] interests, for it is a major cause of instability in the Gulf, invites an increased Soviet role, and sustains Iranian expansionism. Therefore it must be brought to an end quickly.

For ending the war the Security Council is the preferred forum and an embargo on arms for Iran (if Soviet cooperation can be secured) the expedient most often suggested. In the Gulf it is the task of the United States Middle East Force (commanded in October 1987 by Rear-Admiral Harold Bernsen) to ensure 'freedom of navigation for US-flagged vessels'. And, in the Indian Ocean, there are carrier battle-groups to 'limit Soviet influence and presence'.[24] As Admiral Watkins said in his exposition of the Maritime Strategy:

We now maintain a continual presence in the Indian Ocean . . . our operating tempo has been about 20% higher than during the Vietnam War . . . in this age of violent peace, the Navy is on the front lines already.[25]

Whether this is a prudent precaution, a deployment likely to prove useful on the outbreak of total war, is not a question that need be discussed in this chapter. Two, sometimes three, carrier battle-groups did not spend all those years in the Indian Ocean without rather more in mind than the political application of limited naval force.

That very different endeavour is what happens in the Gulf itself. Even there the naval powers have sometimes been criticised for provoking the belligerents while protecting only the small minority of merchant vessels flying their own flags. On 17 December 1987, for instance, the destroyer USS CHANDLER merely watched while Iranian speedboats attacked the ISLAND TRANSPORTER, setting the ship on fire and machine-gunning the crew who abandoned her. Because the freighter flew the Maldives flag, she had no claim to protection. Even her cargo was destined for another neutral – India.[26]

It was the British frigate SCYLLA (a ship we shall encounter again in a later chapter) that broke the pattern before 1987 was over. On 24 December she protected the Liberian tanker EASTERN POWER from Iranian speedboats; on the 25th she rescued sailors from the burning Korean freighter HYUNDAI No. 7. She was assisted by the American frigate ELROD. The next day various foreign ships joined the convoy SCYLLA was escorting. On 30 December the destroyer HMS YORK protected the Panamanian WORLD SPRING and the Liberian WORLD PROGRESS. These developments came too late to prevent 1987 ending with a record total of attacks on merchant ships – 178.[27]

Nor did events in the first half of 1988 suggest that the pattern of naval involvement in the Gulf had undergone any major change. Merchant shipping continued to suffer at the hands of both belligerents. In April the mining of the frigate USS SAMUEL B. ROBERTS provoked major American reprisals against Iran, who lost three warships in the fighting that followed, including the frigate SAHAND. International cooperation to keep the sea lanes open seemed as far away as ever and maritime depredation had not obviously improved the prospects of either Iran or Iraq. Sailors could only console themselves with the reflection that worse things happened on land.

Keeping the sea lanes open is one of those phrases that roll easily off the well-lubricated tongues of political leaders. Its translation into specific orders to naval officers always excites controversy. During the Spanish Civil War, for instance, Admiral Chatfield, then First Sea Lord, deprecated the provision of British naval protection for merchant ships, whether these were carrying food to Spain or children to safety. He wanted to avoid the least risk of precipitating a wider war for which the Royal Navy was not yet ready. In some ways he had a stronger case than now exists in the Gulf. Italian soldiers and German airmen were already fighting in Spain; Italian aircraft and submarines were sinking ships in the Mediterranean. Nevertheless Chatfield was overruled by the British government of the day and, if no wider war resulted, this may have been partly because German admirals were not ready either.[28]

Today there is no outside participation in the fighting ashore, nor are the naval powers ideologically committed to either belligerent, as some were in the Spanish Civil War. But nor is there much echo of the caution – Cordell Hull, then US Secretary of State, called it 'moral aloofness'[29] – that had once caused the United States Government to withdraw its warships from the coasts of Spain as well as prohibiting the despatch of munitions or the departure of volunteers to Spain.

In 1987 there was arguably greater readiness than in 1937 to play with fire and less constructive application of limited naval force. To an extent that may surprise some British admirals sceptical of the utility of history to naval officers, some features of that earlier period recurred half a century later: problems with mines and with shore facilities for rest and recreation; reflagging of merchant ships in quest of naval protection; complaints that allies were doing less than they could to help; air attacks on ships; retaliatory bombardment. Only the humanitarian concern which kept the Royal Navy so busy, even requiring them to escort Spanish ships carrying Spanish children to safety, has found no echo in today's Persian Gulf.[30]

The influence of recent events on the future of gunboat diplomacy is more than usually uncertain. Until the Gulf War ends or escalates, we cannot hope to predict what lessons the admirals or the diplomats or the analysts of the 1990s may draw from the experience of the 1980s. The final result is likely to colour the events that preceded it. But the wise men will waste their time if they merely conclude that a clear political objective would have permitted a more effective application of limited naval force: in the protection of merchant shipping, for instance. Naturally such a conclusion would be fully justified, but, in the real world, motives are always liable to be mixed.

The most that can safely be said while the outcome of the conflict remains uncertain, is that the 1980s in the Persian Gulf have seen more outside warships hovering for more years on the fringes of someone else's war than has happened since the Spanish Civil War ended in 1939. Whether these neutral navies did much good or harm by their presence remains to be seen, but they have again demonstrated, beyond the possibility of doubt, the vigorous survival of gunboat diplomacy. During what remains of the century other navies may be active in different seas, but there is only one discernible threat to the future of a practice that has flourished and proliferated for a hundred years. This is not – would that it were – détente or the international law of the sea or peace on earth, but total war and the end of navies: in the northern hemisphere at least.

6 Showing the Flag

> In the harbours or roads of foreign princes . . . the Commanders
> of his Majesty's ships are . . . carefully to inform themselves how
> flags of the same quality of other princes have been saluted there,
> and to insist upon being saluted with as great respect and advantage
> as any such flags have been in that place . . . .
>
> By his Majesty's command
>
> SAMUEL PEPYS[1]

Showing the flag was a serious matter in the seventeenth century.
The articles of peace ending the Third Dutch War in 1674, for
instance, required the Dutch 'to strike flag and lower topsail to the
King's Jack between Finisterre and Norway'.[2] Not until 1806 was the
duty of naval commanders to enforce salutes in the British Seas
omitted from the Naval Instructions issued by the Admiralty.[3] Nor
have other nations, in their moments of naval ascendancy, been
reluctant to substitute their own emblem when echoing the sentiment
of:

> The meteor flag of England
> Shall yet terrific burn.[4]

Naturally the concept has undergone considerable modification
over the centuries. Navies, even nations, have on the whole become
less arrogant as the potential disadvantages of provocative behaviour
have become more obvious. Enforcing salutes no longer makes sense
for most modern warships, which are acutely vulnerable if the distance
is small enough for the flag to be unmistakable. If showing the flag is
still a frequent, even an important naval activity, the expression must
nowadays be given a rather more metaphorical interpretation. In
these pages, however, no conduct will be described as showing the
flag unless it involves the presence of a warship.

Showing the flag is not the same as gunboat diplomacy. That
practice is always intended, however mistakenly, to secure some
advantage or to avert actual loss. Even the expressive use of limited
naval force, in which warships are moved or deployed merely as a
political gesture, as an alternative to effective action or an outlet for
emotion, is related to some specific dispute. Showing the flag can be
no more than a general reminder of the existence of the navy

concerned. It is not always a friendly reminder, but there is no intention of threatening or using force, seldom much expectation of immediate results. Showing the flag is the naval equivalent of the ceremonial and symbolic practices of diplomacy.

The customs of the two professions have another feature in common. It is not of the first importance, but it has to be mentioned, for it excites outsiders and their criticism irritates insiders. A degree of ritual and parade is attached, even today, to the conduct of diplomacy. The cynical regard this as the merest pretext for ensuring that diplomats enjoy a higher standard of living than civil servants. The visits to foreign ports that showing the flag often requires do provide sailors with rest, recreation and some of the amenities of foreign travel. These are aids to naval recruiting. In neither case does the agreeable flavour of the icing detract from the solid nourishment of the cake.

What is shown may properly be distinguished either as a friendly or an unfriendly flag, but the underlying objective is much the same, even if the immediate purpose and, still more, the techniques employed are different. 'They that have power to hurt, and will do none' is the message that showing the flag conveys, but the distribution of emphasis between 'power to hurt' and 'will do none' can vary greatly. At one extreme a display of naval power may reassure allies, at another enemies may be intimidated, but there is a large spectrum of signals in between.

SHOWING AN UNFRIENDLY FLAG

Sending warships where they are not wanted is often done in gunboat diplomacy in order to score a point in a particular dispute. HMS VICTORIOUS asserted the right of the Royal Navy – perhaps trailing Britannia's cloak in the process – to effect an innocent passage of the Lombok Straits in 1964 during Britain's 'confrontation' with Indonesia. The US Sixth Fleet have repeatedly defied the Libyan claim to exclusive rights in the Gulf of Sirte. But flags may be flaunted even in the absence of any specific dispute and without warranting the wisp of an assumption that identifiable advantage was expected.

The United States Navy, for instance, makes quite a practice of coat-trailing in or near Soviet territorial waters. No lawyer could have faulted it in December 1984, when two US battle-groups, including the aircraft carriers CARL VINSON and MIDWAY, sailed within

50 miles of Vladivostok. If a hundred Soviet aircraft were scrambled, this may have been either a prudent or a nervous reaction. It was not juridically inevitable.

In March 1986, when the Soviet Union protested against the much closer approach of the cruiser USS YORKTOWN and the destroyer USS CARON to the Crimean coast, the Russians may have been on stronger legal ground. In February 1988 the US Department of Defense even admitted that YORKTOWN and CARON, those connoisseurs of Crimea's scenic beauties, had been asserting the right of innocent passage through Russian territorial waters when bumped by Russian warships in the Black Sea on the 12th. The Russians, who conceded that the frigate BEZZAVETNY and her consort had tried to 'shoulder' the intruders out to sea, rejected American claims to innocence and described the manoeuvres of YORKTOWN and CARON as 'military provocation'.[5] They had been equally indignant, in May 1987, at the manoeuvres of the nuclear-powered cruiser USS ARKANSAS, a third of the way round the globe, off the Kamchatka peninsula.

The purpose of such manoeuvres is never fully explained. They may have an intelligence function: to ascertain, by provocation, the state of Soviet alertness on that particular coast; the nature of Soviet radar coverage; perhaps even Soviet response times. It is conceivable that there is a political objective: to assert the right of the US Navy to sail where they please; to manifest their confidence that American warships need fear no challenge to their freedom of movement. Training could also be a motive: to accustom officers and men to discharging their duties in a potentially hazardous environment. All that is difficult to imagine is how these ships could be expected to gain advantage or avert loss in any specific and identifiable dispute.

Much the same might be said of Soviet naval activities off the coast of Sweden since the stranding of one of their submarines in October 1981 outside the Swedish naval base of Karlskrona. This saga is particularly baffling, because most of the facts are in dispute. Only one Soviet submarine was discovered, identified, photographed: not only on the surface, but aground. The Swedish Navy was unable to produce enough evidence to convince Western experts that all the 95 submarine 'sightings' of the next three years were genuine.[6] If some of them were, what was the Russian motive? It cannot have been obvious or related to any specific dispute. Yet, in October 1987, General Gustafsson, the Swedish Supreme Commander, maintained that submarine incursions into Swedish waters were still continuing.[7]

In April 1984 the Soviet helicopter carrier LENINGRAD and the destroyer UDALOY conducted anti-submarine exercises with ships of the Cuban navy in the Gulf of Mexico and within 75 miles of the coast of the United States. Although these manoeuvres, which attracted some attention in the American press, were legally unobjectionable, no Russian could feel much surprise if, in Washington, LENINGRAD seemed to be showing an unfriendly flag.

The Super Powers are more inclined than others to such manifestations, but they are not entirely alone. Although discreet intelligence-gathering or specifically motivated gunboat diplomacy tend to pre-empt the efforts of lesser navies, there are occasional outbursts of exuberance. It is hard to see, for instance, what Spain hoped to gain by sending the carrier DEDALO into the territorial waters of Gibraltar in March 1986 and flying off a couple of helicopters. There had, of course, for generations been a dispute, so Spaniards might have been content to reply for their admiral:

> He only does it to annoy
> Because he knows it teases.

As a classification of naval activity, showing an unfriendly flag is both controversial and imprecise. The government that sends ships where they are not wanted will rarely admit to acting mischievously. A favourite excuse is participation in a naval exercise. This can sometimes – for instance the Iranian exercise called Operation Martyrdom in August 1987 – be the merest pretext for harassment: a form of gunboat diplomacy. Alternatively, what was originally conceived as a form of training can be exploited to present a veiled threat. Hervé Coutau-Bégarie has argued that both the Chinese and the Japanese so interpreted certain aspects of the Russian exercise Okean II in 1975.[8]

A sinister paradox makes most exercises seem less menacing. Although designed to mimic warlike operations against a foe whose identity is barely veiled, the real 'enemy' is seldom disturbed by this evidence of a hostility he takes for granted. Tension rises only when the location of the exercise, occasionally some other factor, suggests that the parade of sham belligerence conceals a peacetime purpose. Such an exercise was the American Operation Amber in 1981 which, as explained in Chapter 4, carried a menacing message for the government of Grenada.

Perhaps no navy is assigned the role of 'enemy' in as many foreign exercises as that of the Soviet Union, usually described with minimal tact as 'Orange'. Naturally any Russian tolerance tends to be grudging. In September 1986 *Pravda* wrote:

> The US fleet is on manoeuvres in the immediate vicinity of the Soviet Union – from the Northern Sea and the Baltic to the Far East. Of course these 'shows of muscle' do not frighten our country. But . . . what would happen if the Warsaw Pact countries mounted similar manoeuvres around the United States?[9]

It is an interesting sidelight on the continuing importance of a visible flag that in neither Super Power do the media display equal concern at the lurking and constant presence of the other's far more dangerous strategic submarines.

Nevertheless, *Pravda* was for once not exaggerating. In 1986 the Atlantic Command (to mention no other) of the US Navy held over thirty exercises, many involving allied navies as well. Two of the more important, Anchor Express and Northern Wedding (in which 150 ships took part) were concerned with the reinforcement of Norway against hypothetical Russian attack.[10] The Soviet Navy, which had conducted major exercises in and around the Norwegian Sea in 1984 and 1985, were less active in 1986. Naturally, however, they kept a close eye on what NATO was up to.

An understanding attitude towards naval manoeuvres is rarer still in countries with few naval pretensions of their own. A reflection of their views may be found in the *Study on the Naval Arms Race* published by the United Nations in 1985:

> in the opinion of non-aligned and neutral states, naval exercises and training of this nature are more likely to unsettle international security than to consolidate it . . . particularly in the case of large-scale exercises, especially if world-wide, which are clearly designed to create exercise conditions and incidents close to those anticipated in the event of actual conflict.[11]

It is natural that rehearsals for naval war should excite only repugnance in those incapable of significant participation. To the naval powers, it can be argued, such manoeuvres may actually seem less objectionable than those which cannot plausibly be represented as practising the likely operations of a hypothetical, hopefully distant war. The ears of admirals are disturbed, not soothed, to hear that:

> Peace hath her victories
> No less renowned than war.

In 1986, for instance, there were two other American naval

penetrations of the Black Sea beside the YORKTOWN/CARON cruise that attracted Russian protests. Yet, Maritime Strategy or no Maritime Strategy, it is hard to imagine the conflict in which this sea could become a naval theatre of war between the Super Powers. What hypothetical operation could the battleship NEW JERSEY have been rehearsing when, in company with the cruisers LONG BEACH and VINCENNES as well as a couple of destroyers, she crossed the Sea of Okhotsk in September 1986? Should we infer from the Baltic cruise of the USS THORN and the USS MOINESTER in October 1986 that the Maritime Strategy has revived Churchill's Plan Catherine, which the British Admiralty rejected in 1939?[12]

These are improbable conjectures. Perhaps the US Navy were simply showing, as they often do to the Russians, an unfriendly flag. Too little has been published, by way of explanation, by any of the naval powers addicted to this practice, either to justify or to refute the notion that its likely benefits outweigh the risk that it might one day precipitate an unintended conflict.

SHOWING A FRIENDLY FLAG

It is, of course, the eyes of the beholder that decide the nature of the flag. In 1984 the Cubans may well have thought LENINGRAD was flying a friendly flag. There are more ways of conveying goodwill or reassurance than there are of indicating hostility. Once the recipient of a naval message senses ill-will, the only variable he is likely to notice is the strength of the signal. But friendly flags are available in various patterns. There is more than one meaning just as there is more than one kind of audience.

Naturally no two cases are ever quite the same, but the categories can be simplified. When warships are sent across the sea to show a friendly flag, the intended recipient of the message may be an ally, a neutral or even an undeclared enemy. The chosen audience may be narrowly professional – another navy and its associated defence establishment; or it may be as wide as public opinion. The theme may be power or smartness or simple friendliness or some kind of mixture.

For planners the simplest problem – always remembering that every case is different and needs individual attention – is often the official visit to a rival naval base. Any straightforward manifestation of power is usually excluded. Such visits take place only by prior agreement and the host government would not accept a ship or ships liable to overawe. Nor would the visiting navy want to expose its latest and best to close inspection. When Rear-Admiral Kalinin made a rare Soviet naval visit to an American port – Boston in May 1975 – he took only two destroyers (BOYKIY and ZHGUCHIY). The aircraft carriers went to the ports of Russia's allies or clients. The US Navy followed the same pattern, sending the destroyers LEAHY and TATNALL (also with a Rear-Admiral) to Leningrad.[13]

Nor is it rewarding on such occasions to expend much effort on an unconvincing display of friendship. The fellow-travellers or the dissidents to whom it might appeal lack political influence. Smartness, on the other hand, will impress the rival navy without disclosing any secrets. In 1934 a German visit to Portsmouth managed to dazzle the British officer who reported it in the *Naval Review*:

> The long unbroken line of men on the forecastle of the KÖNIGSBERG – perfectly dressed and sized – so that the lines corresponded with the sheer of the deck itself was especially striking.

Smartness is equally desirable in other kinds of visit, but the emphasis is not always on paintwork, crisp uniforms, the bearing or the marching of sailors on parade. In 1902 the Tsar of Russia arranged for his Baltic Fleet to give the visiting Kaiser Wilhelm II of Germany a display of gunnery. In 1952 the carrier USS CORAL SEA embarked President Tito of Yugoslavia to witness an equivalent manifestation of power at sea. In 1979 the Soviet carrier MINSK and amphibious warfare ship IVAN ROGOV showed the government of South Yemen what they could do. But ship-handling is always important. Collisions can impair the political advantages of joining in manoeuvres with allied navies. Worse still, the American frigate McCANDLESS actually managed to run aground on a visit to Helsinki in 1982.[14]

If the exchange of naval visits between rivals is now so rare, this is probably the result of two modern diseases: ideology and espionage. From 1897 onwards it was increasingly admitted that, in the words of Admiral Tirpitz, 'for Germany the most dangerous naval enemy at the present time is England.'[15] Yet the two navies continued to exchange visits, for which royal occasions and the annual yachting regattas at Cowes and Kiel furnished useful opportunities. Relations between the British and Japanese navies languished after the Anglo-Japanese Alliance ended in 1922, but the British China Squadron were hospitably received on a visit to Japan in 1933.[16] The decline of monarchy has been no gain for peace, but the Soviet Navy did try to revive a better tradition by sending a cruiser to the Coronation Naval Review at Spithead in 1953.

Perhaps the British must take some of the blame if the revival failed to catch on. In October 1955, when the Russian cruiser SVERDLOV visited Spithead, her hull is said to have been secretly scrutinised by British frogmen. An attempt to repeat the operation when the cruiser ORDJONIKIDZE came to Portsmouth in April 1956 for the visit to Britain of the Soviet leaders Bulganin and Khruschev resulted in the embarrassing death of a frogman – Commander Crabbe.[17] Of course, British warships visiting Russian ports received similar attentions, even if their reprisals were less drastic. It is hard to believe anyone ever obtained intelligence worth a fraction of the political price they paid.

The friendly flag, however, is mainly displayed to allies, clients or neutrals. In 1979, for instance, the Russian aircraft carrier MINSK made a remarkable voyage from Nikolayev in the Black Sea, where she had commissioned, halfway round the world to join the Soviet Pacific Fleet. While on passage she called at Luanda, where the President of embattled Angola went on board to contemplate this visible manifestation of the power of his Soviet patrons. Mozambique, on the other side of Africa, was a less steadfast client, but well worth a call by MINSK. South Yemen, as earlier mentioned, was treated to a display of air power and amphibious operations. Once in the Pacific, MINSK paid more than one visit, during the 1980s, to the ports of two other Soviet clients: Vietnam and North Korea.

A government confronting a foreign threat will often welcome the visit of an allied capital ship as a useful reminder – to their own citizens as much as to their enemies – of the power which they hope they can summon to their assistance. Timing is important. In 1984 MINSK, together with IVAN ROGOV, joined Vietnamese ships for an amphibious exercise when Vietnam had come under renewed pressure from China. In the same year, when elections were held in El Salvador (a country regarded by its rulers and their American friends as menaced from outside), the carrier USS AMERICA, together with the destroyers WILLIAM V. PRATT and DEWEY, arrived to inspire electors with enough confidence to cast the right vote.

Purely internal disturbances, on the other hand, may not provide a suitable setting in which to show the flag. When rioting erupted in Karachi, causing 50 deaths in November 1986 and another 100 in December, the Government of Pakistan asked the Government of the United Kingdom to cancel the planned visit to Karachi of the

British carrier ILLUSTRIOUS and frigate BEAVER. A display of power could only have been provocative and one of smartness would have been irrelevant if not unnoticed. As for friendship, its cultivation demands a calmer climate.

Most friendly visits, indeed, do not take place against a background of conflict or crisis. October 1986, when the large anti-submarine warfare ships OCHAKOV and KRASNY KAVKAZ paid a 'friendly official visit' to Havana (the twenty-sixth since 1969), was an almost tranquil moment in the turbulent history of Cuba.[18]

An auspicious anniversary is often favoured as one way of striking the right note. Forty years after the departure from Portsmouth of the allied expeditionary forces under the supreme command of General Eisenhower, there arrived in June 1984 at the same port the nuclear-powered aircraft carrier USS DWIGHT D. EISENHOWER, together with the cruiser MISSISSIPPI (also nuclear-powered) and the destroyer SCOTT. This occasion was notable for more than its imaginative planning. It demonstrated American readiness to expose some of their most modern and sophisticated ships to British inspection and British willingness, which is not shared by every ally of the United States, to accept the presence of ships that were nuclear-powered as well as nuclear-capable.

Tact is naturally required when choosing anniversaries. The example of the British Admiralty – inviting the Free French Navy to join in the 1940 celebration of Trafalgar Day – is not one to be widely imitated. The Royal Navy were rightly left out of the party in 1981, when President Mitterrand gave President Reagan luncheon aboard the DE GRASSE in Chesapeake Bay. The French destroyer was, after all, named after the commander who had successfully out-manoeuvred the British Admiral Graves in that very bay just 200 years earlier. The results of that French success – American victory ashore at Yorktown and later in the entire War of Independence – were better suited to bilateral celebration.

The advantage of focusing on a historical occasion is that this provides (if carefully explained to the media) an appropriate theme for the visit: our two nations stood together then and, if need be, will again. Such sentimental analogies are often politically more effective – more plausible, even – than any attempt to expound the naval strategy of the alliance. In the television era any diplomatic gesture intended to influence public opinion must be tailored to the cameras. Freshly painted warships, their flags streaming in the wind, and young, smartly-uniformed sailors offer better 'photo-opportunities' than the forced smiles of politicians and diplomats.

Historical symbolism is less appropriate in naval visits to neutrals, particularly to those nations who make a political point of their neutrality. The 800th anniversary of the city of Cork was a good opportunity for Rear-Admiral Gromov to visit the port in the destroyer SOOBRAZITELNY only because the Russian navy could not be blamed for any of the misfortunes of those eight rather unhappy centuries. Irish history is singularly rich in incidents better not commemorated. The battle of Bantry Bay, for instance, or the relief of Londonderry are memories the Royal Navy would be rash to revive.

Naval visits to neutral countries, more than any others, require diplomatic advice in their conception and diplomatic cooperation in their planning and execution. So much depends on factors with which naval officers cannot be expected to be conversant: the political situation in the country to be visited; the customs, traditions and prejudices of the natives; even the local climate and holiday seasons.

It can, of course, be argued that a naval visit to a neutral is politically less important than one to an ally, and less sensitive than one to a rival, just as a routine visit matters less than one in time of crisis. Even if this were always true, there is also much that can go wrong. In an allied port one can at least hope that friendly naval officers, politicians, officials, occasionally even the media, will excuse or cover up any blunders the visitors may make. Neutrals tend to be less indulgent when a manoeuvre is bungled, the mayor is left off the guest-list, the ship's band plays the wrong anthem or sailors create a drunken disturbance ashore. Even clients can be touchy. Gorshkov's failure to call on the Egyptian admiral at Alexandria may have played a part in the Soviet Navy's eventual loss of their facilities in Egypt.[19]

Naval visits can, and naval visits usually do, make a better impression than such anecdotes might suggest. A British warship in a foreign port creates an image of efficiency, smartness and friendly hospitality that helps to soften, perhaps to dissolve, foreign memories of London Airport, of British package tourists, even of British football fans. The folk-dancers amusing the guests aboard a Soviet warship, the discreetly behaved Russian sailors ashore (each formed party led by a trusted petty officer) help foreigners to forget the Gulag and the KGB. These effects are not achieved by chance or because every girl loves a sailor. When they happen, they are the result of advance information, intelligent planning, good diplomatic liaison and the discipline and hard work of officers and men.

Thereafter, naval visits are frequently fun, for the sailors ashore no less than for their guests on board.

THE CONTEMPORARY FLAG

In the last quarter of the twentieth century there is a tendency to turn a sceptical eye on the continuing validity of traditional practices. Many more examples could have been offered – this chapter has scarcely scratched the surface of the subject – to demonstrate that navies do still show the flag. But is it still worth the trouble required and the international tension occasionally caused?

Naturally, as the legendary Chinaman is supposed to have remarked earlier this century when discussing the consequences of the French Revolution, it is still too soon to say. Showing the flag, friendly or other, seldom has the obvious motives or the prompt results of naval action in war or gunboat diplomacy. It is part of the continuing, flickering, rather symbolic film of international relations. The pattern may be easier for future historians to discern than it is for us to guess. Meanwhile showing the flag provides navies with peacetime occupation; helps to justify their cost to taxpayers; is often thought – by diplomats and politicians as well as naval officers – to be useful. It is likely to last as long as navies.

7 Estate Management at Sea

[The] Sovereign, as Lord of the Waste, is said to be Lord also of the British territorial waters and the soil beneath them. – HIGH COURT OF BOMBAY[1]

The rights and responsibilities of a state in the waters off its coast can usefully be divided into sovereignty, good order and resource enjoyment. – HILL[2]

[The] United States has some forty overlapping agencies concerned with the offshore estate, the British over twenty. – TILL[3]

Most navies are not ocean-going, either in their plans for war or in their peacetime routine. They are concerned with the adjacent seas, which they may call territorial, or historic, or contiguous or archipelagic, or a continental shelf or an exclusive economic zone. The expanse of sea over which various kinds of jurisdiction are claimed may extend between three (the minimum) and 200 (the usual maximum) miles from the coast, but resort to such ingenious concepts as low-tide elevations, measurement from submerged reefs and atolls, and compound bays, effectively cushions international lawyers against the risks of unemployment. And even ocean-going navies may have to spend some of their time enforcing or challenging the rules derived from such pleasing fancies.

Some navies, of course, prefer to delegate the inshore responsibilities defined by Admiral Hill. The Canadian Coast Guard has hitherto had more ships and sailors than the Canadian Navy, but 1987 saw the publication of an ambitious plan for naval expansion. The Japanese Maritime Safety Agency is larger than the Canadian Coast Guard – larger, indeed, than many navies – but not as large as the navy of Japan. The United States Coast Guard has more ships and sailors than the navies of either West or East Germany, than those of Greece, Sweden, Yugoslavia, Egypt, Australia, Indonesia, of either North or South Korea, or of Argentina.[4] And the US Coast Guard, by international standards, is rather heavily armed.

In the Soviet Union the emphasis is a little different. Coastal defence has always been a major task for the Soviet Navy, many of whose ships seem mainly designed for inshore work. Nevertheless, the Maritime Border Guards of the KGB have a substantial fleet of their own. They need it, for they have a double task.

> The following shall be deemed violators of the state boundary of the USSR . . . persons who are discovered on means of navigation, or swimming, in territorial and internal sea waters of the USSR . . . if they are illegally attempting to leave their limits.[5]

Altogether 105 states maintain navies, many of them very small and amounting to no more than a coast guard. Of these 105 states 43 have both a navy and a separate sea-going force called coast guard or fishery patrol or maritime police or something similar. This practice is particularly prevalent among those states maintaining substantial navies. Brazil and Britain are notable exceptions, though both navies have ships with specifically coastal functions.[6] Allotting such duties to different organisations, often answering not to the ministry of defence but to another department, may be prompted by tradition or by administrative convenience or even by the ancient principle of dividing the control of armed force in order to maintain the primacy of political authority.

Vessels employed on coastal patrols have very various duties, many of which do not involve the use or threat of force. The US Coast Guard, for instance, sent eleven cutters (which can be quite large vessels) to render assistance after the 1965 collision between the liners ANDREA DORIA and STOCKHOLM off the eastern coast of North America.[7] In 1979, when storms overwhelmed 24 yachts competing in the Fastnet Race:

> A massive rescue operation was mounted, which included the British and Irish coast guards and life boat services, innumerable fishing and merchant vessels, the Dutch destroyer OVERIJSSEL, the British frigates BROADSWORD and SCYLLA, the patrol boat ANGLESEY (among others) and maritime aircraft from the Fleet Air Arm, the Irish Air Corps and the Royal Air Force.[8]

Warships and coastguard vessels are frequently involved in rescues and other humanitarian tasks, as are policemen ashore, both because they tend to be available and because they usually have larger and better-trained crews. But that is not their main function.

Nor is it the subject of this book, which is concerned with the employment of navies in *violent* peace. The vessels which states deploy to patrol their adjacent seas may have functions that are

strictly defensive, regulatory, law-enforcing. Only occasionally is it
their job actually to enlarge the jurisdiction of their state – as when
HMS VIDAL claimed Rockall in 1955, thus permitting an eventual
extension of the British continental shelf by 50 000 square miles.[9]
Nevertheless these ships represent both the authority and the power
of the state. They are usually armed and not always lightly. Their
essential function – and the one to be considered in this chapter – is
that of policing the adjacent sea. How they do it – and to some
extent why – is worth a glance, but there is not world enough nor
time to examine all the administrative agencies that direct their
activities nor the legal pretexts they so often invoke.

SOVEREIGNTY

Whatever the nature or extent, let alone the legal grounds, of the
rights a state may claim in, over or under the adjacent sea, these
rights must usually be upheld against those, whether states or persons,
who might otherwise defy or deny them. The practical need for
enforcement is obvious, but so, it seems, is the legal requirement.
The International Court held in 1951 that

> the only convincing evidence of State practice is to be found in
> seizures, where the coastal State asserts its sovereignty over the
> waters in question.

As Professor O'Connell subsequently explained, 'mere claim, even
if embodied in legislation, is insufficient'.[10]

That is why the Argentine Navy so often seizes, sinks or simply
fires on fishing vessels – Bulgarian, Japanese, Korean, Polish and
Spanish during 1986 alone – in the disputed waters between Argentina
and the Falklands.[11] They want – without incurring any undue risk –
to assert a claim they failed to maintain in war.

Most fishery protection, of course, is a function of what Admiral
Hill calls 'resource enjoyment', but the Argentines are prosecuting
one of those disputes where sovereignty is almost certainly a more
important consideration. A purer example is the long-standing dispute
between Canada and the United States concerning sovereignty over
the North West Passage through the waters of Canada's Arctic
archipelago. In 1970, for instance, after the transit of the North West
Passage by the American oil tanker MANHATTAN, Canada passed the
Arctic Waters Pollution Act and assumed the legal right to regulate

shipping in Arctic waters. The voyage of the icebreaker POLAR SEA, which the US Coast Guard, *not* the US navy, sent all the way from Lancaster Sound in the east to Beaufort Sea in the west in August 1985, renewed the American challenge to claims which Canada has often made, but so far has failed to enforce. Canadians were particularly annoyed by the POLAR SEA, but hers was actually the ninth transit by vessels of either the US Coast Guard or the US Navy since 1957.[12]

It is interesting to contrast the difficulty experienced by Canada with Soviet success in asserting a similar claim. In August 1967 the United States Government notified the Soviet Foreign Ministry that two icebreakers of the US Coast Guard – a service whose extraterritorial ambitions found simultaneous expression by the despatch of a substantial contingent to take part in the war in Vietnam – proposed to pass through the Volkitsky Straits between the Kara and Laptev seas to the north of Russia. When informed that

> the straits consituted Soviet territorial waters and that passage of the ships through the straits would be a violation of Soviet frontiers

the Coast Guard abandoned the plan.[13] As President Theodore Roosevelt once remarked:

> speak softly and carry a big stick; you will go far.[14]

Perhaps the commonest cause of dispute concerning maritime sovereignty stems from the right claimed by certain coastal states of requiring foreign warships to seek prior permission before entering waters regarded as territorial. In 1983, for instance, the Soviet research vessel AYU-DAG was fined 8000 kroner for entering Oslo fjord without permission, then escorted out of Norwegian territorial waters by a Norwegian warship.[15] That was also the issue at stake when the Soviet Union protested at American incursions or the Scandinavians complained of infestation by Soviet submarines. Naturally the facts of any particular case can be even more controversial than the law. Some of the published submarine statistics, for instance, are hard to believe – 211 sightings in Norwegian waters since 1969; 143 in Swedish waters since 1962.[16] If both Norwegians and Swedes have dropped depth-charges, this is better proof of readiness to enforce their rights than of the actual presence of submarines.

The Libyans did what they could in the Gulf of Sirte but, whether or not they had a case in international law, they were unable to prevent or repel the intrusions of the US Sixth Fleet. The acid test of sovereignty at sea is the ability to exclude others. This may entail the use of force, even violence: Albanian mining of the Corfu Straits in 1946 or North Korean seizure of the USS PUEBLO in 1968.[17] If no force is available, mere assertion – the 1971 declaration by the governments of Indonesia and Malaysia that the Straits of Malacca and Singapore were 'not international straits' – cuts little ice.[18]

Fortunately most claims to sovereignty over adjacent seas are no longer seriously disputed. International agreement has often followed, however reluctantly, the assertive naval flag. When dispute persists, various expedients are available and have on occasion been employed by coastal states desirous of repelling foreign warships or other intruding vessels: minefields, coastal artillery or missiles, military aircraft or warships. The most flexible defence is provided by warships, which are better able to identify, challenge and, if need be, expressly warn the intruder before opening fire.

A warship is usually better placed for the classic gambit of a shot across the bows and better able to restrict the use of force to the minimum actually necessary. Sometimes – as in the Icelandic 'cod wars' between 1958 and 1976 – aggressive manoeuvring may obviate the need to open fire at all. In August 1987 the confrontation between the Colombian frigate CALDAS and a superior force of Venezuelan warships supported by aircraft lasted over a week in the disputed waters of the Gulf of Venezuela before the Colombian Government were induced to withdraw their ship.[19] The price to be paid for these advantages (which often include the chance to capture rather than sink) is that warships on coastal patrol are themselves vulnerable to a hostile or merely trigger-happy intruder. Peace must be very violent before this risk is no longer worth running.

GOOD ORDER

Threats to good order, as opposed to challenges to sovereignty, in the adjacent seas are less likely to emanate from foreign states. Ordinary merchant ships may become a source of danger if they are carelessly or incompetently navigated; in unseaworthy condition; liable to cause pollution by the deliberate or accidental discharge of noxious substances. Fishermen sometimes combine to block a strait or obstruct the entrance to a harbour. Spanish and Portuguese fishermen used their boats to do that at the mouth of the Guadiana river in November 1986. French fishermen, exasperated by exclusion from their traditional fishing grounds a result of the legal ingenuity with which the British had drafted the Territorial Sea Act of 1987, blocked the ports of Boulogne, Calais, Dieppe and Dunkirk against cross-Channel ferries at the end of October 1987.[20] Although that blockade only lasted two days, it bore some fruit. The British Government allowed the fishermen to use the disputed waters pending negotiations and, two months later, the Commission of the European Economic Community began legal proceedings against the British Government.[21] Once again lawyers followed where ships had led.

Smugglers, criminals, pirates and terrorists may operate in waters over which the coastal state claims jurisdiction. There are often good practical reasons for policing adjacent waters. In October 1987, for instance, the presence off Blackpool of the minesweeper HMS CUXTON, with a detachment on board from the Special Boat Squadron of the Royal Marines, was intended to protect the annual conference of the British Conservative Party (attended by members of the British Government) from seaborne attack. In Britain this was an unusual precaution, prompted by threats from the Irish Republican Army.[22] But a Finnish warship anchored off the waterfront presidential palace at Helsinki when a coup d'état was feared in 1948. In the 1970s the Soviet Navy did President Sekou Touré of Guinea the same service at Conakry.

The concept of the police powers of the coastal state naturally becomes contentious if the maritime sovereignty of that state is itself in dispute. In 1986 Indonesia and Malaysia agreed to increase their joint patrols in what they did not admit to be the 'international' Strait of Malacca 'to prevent smuggling, drug trafficking, illegal fishing and pollution from tankers'.[23] If we leave aside fishing, always a controversial issue and one to be considered in the next section of this chapter, these are worthy purposes. As long as the transgressors are Indonesian or Malaysian or nationals of mild and peace-loving states, the exercise of these police functions may pass unchallenged. But what happens if a passing tanker under the flag of a Super Power pollutes the Strait?

A large tanker reluctant to interrupt its passage is not easily stopped by any warship without the use of more force than most navies care to contemplate against a Super Power. On the other hand, many Britons who remember the damage done by the stranding of the tanker TORREY CANYON in 1967, and many Frenchmen recalling the pollution spread in 1978 by the AMOCO CADIZ, would argue for more control by the littoral states not merely over the navigation of oil tankers in their waters, but over other factors affecting the ability of these vessels to avoid pollution. There are, of course, over twenty major international straits and as many countries with a plausible claim to control them.

Nor is oil the only potential pollutant that ships can carry. Some countries object to the presence in their waters of ships that are nuclear-propelled or which carry nuclear weapons. New Zealand has already quarrelled with her allies on this issue. As foreign warships have no pressing need to visit New Zealand, this dispute has not led to actual conflict, which might be the result of attempts by a coastal state or states to exclude warships with nuclear reactors or nuclear weapons from important international straits. Denmark did not go to such desperate lengths. Nevertheless, the mere passage by the Danish Parliament in April 1988 of a resolution urging the Government to remind visiting warships 'that for the past thirty years it has been Danish policy not to accept nuclear weapons on Danish territory, including Danish ports' was enough to precipitate a general election in Denmark and weeks of fuss in NATO. In the end, so at least it seemed in June 1988, there was tacit agreement to imitate Nelson's conduct at Copenhagen: 'I really do not see the signal.'

Conflict arising from pollution is not an entirely fanciful notion, even if no formal protest to the United States Government was reported when the nuclear-powered submarine ATLANTA ran aground in the Straits of Gibraltar in 1986. And this is a narrow strait well within the 12-mile territorial sea claimed by both Spain and Morocco, to say nothing of the more debatable pretensions of the British colony of Gibraltar. The Irish Sea is admittedly wider, but either Britain or the Irish Republic might have had cause to complain when another submarine, the USS NATHANAEL GREENE with 16 Poseidon missiles, ran aground on 13 March 1986.[24] It is a safe bet that attempts to police straits are likely to be made in future and to lead to disputes, perhaps even conflicts. The maritime nations will not always accept that the coastal states are solely concerned to preserve their citizens from danger and their shores from pollution. Political or strategic purposes, even the quest for economic advantage, will sometimes be suspected, perhaps rightly suspected.

Few governments, however, always accept the elimination of pollution as an overriding priority. That remarkable organisation, at once private and international, Greenpeace, has managed to get its members arrested by the coastal forces of countries as various as the Soviet Union, Spain, Iceland and Australia. Even if the British

Sovereign can still be rightly regarded as 'Lord of the Waste', the Queen's subjects are nowadays victims as well as perpetrators of the increasingly controversial practice of dumping noxious wastes at sea. This has already caused low-level conflict. In October 1987 Danish fishing vessels in the North Sea surrounded the chemical waste ship VULCANUS II and engaged in battle with hoses. The action was apparently organised by Greenpeace, which said the damage to the ship's propeller (which forced it to return to port) was accidental.[25] One way or the other, the Royal Navy will have another police function to perform.

There are a fair number already: patrolling the coast of Ulster against seaborne gun runners or terrorists, for instance. In 1972, eleven years before Operation Urgent Fury, the Royal Navy gave this task the surprising code-name of Operation Grenada. Many navies have to do this kind of thing and French naval operations during the civil war in Algeria were much more extensive. Various countries have to be prepared to protect offshore oil-rigs against terrorist attack. This has not yet happened in the North Sea (though the frigate HMS SCYLLA was called to the Claymore rig after a bomb-scare in July 1978), but Britain has a quick-reaction force of Royal Marines stationed at Arbroath to cover this contingency. In the modern world few navies can reasonably expect much easing of their ultimate responsibility for good order in coastal waters.

RESOURCE ENJOYMENT

Wherever the sea yields profit, strife is the foam on the crest of the wave. The larger, sharper conflicts belong in the category of gunboat diplomacy: the long feuds over Icelandic fisheries or between Greece and Turkey over submarine oil deposits in the Aegean. But, in 1982–83, the British Ministry of Defence spent £27 million, without firing a shot, on the protection of fisheries and offshore oil and gas installations. In 1981, 1548 vessels were boarded in the British Seas and 43 were convicted of infringing British fishing rights.[26] In 1984 the French Navy fired on the Spanish trawlers BURGOA MENDI and VALLE DE ACHONDO while these were fishing – illegally, the French said – in the Bay of Biscay. Nine Spanish sailors were injured before the two trawlers could be arrested.[27] In 1986, when a fishing agreement with the Soviet Union expired, the South Pacific island state of Kiribati merely asked three Russian trawlers to leave.[28]

There are three main reasons why international disputes over the right to enjoy the resources of the sea are likely to continue to increase.

The first is that many of these resources are already failing to meet the demands made on them. The member states of the European Economic Community caught 883 000 tons of cod in the North East Atlantic during 1970, but only 584 000 tons in 1976. Even in Community waters and after years of efforts at conservation, only 190 000 tons of herring were caught in 1982 compared to some 800 000 a dozen years earlier.

> . . . even the strictest conservation measures on certain declining Community stocks will never be able to replace in full the fishing availability of ten years ago.[29]

Similar problems have been encountered in other seas, where coastal states failed to reach even as much agreement as the Community took quarter of a century to achieve. In 1983 it was possible to write:

> The United States–Canada relationship over the East Coast fisheries is in a state of divorce. Canadian fisherman are banned from fishing in US waters. American fishermen are banned from fishing in Canadian waters.[30]

In April 1988 the French Ambassador to Canada was recalled for consultations after the arrest of the evocatively-named trawler CROIX DE LORRAINE for fishing in waters claimed by both Canada and France.[31]

As for whaling, repeated international conferences have reduced its incidence, but have not brought the practice to an end. In December 1987 *Greenpeace* was still attempting direct action against Japanese whalers, whose departure from Japanese waters had to be protected by the Maritime Safety Agency. The scarcity of petroleum no longer seems as threatening today as it did in the 1970s, when the carrier USS CONSTELLATION was sent to the Persian Gulf (in November 1974) to emphasise that 'Washington will not accept any threat to, or interruption of, the supply of oil from Persian Gulf States.'[32] If the threat is revived by the way in which the war between Iran and Iraq ends, the consequences, as discussed in Chapter 5, might call for measures far beyond the bounds of estate management. If that does not happen, the future might nevertheless bring the return of energy famine from some other cause. Oil platforms out at sea might then strike some planning staff as easier to seize and hold than oil-wells or oil fields inland.

The depletion of existing resources is not the only trend that might generate future conflicts. The second factor pointing in this direction is the widely-held view – it has yet to be tested on a commercial scale – that the sea-bed could furnish a profitable source of rare minerals. Manganese nodules are often mentioned as one example. This idea was taken seriously enough for the 1982 United Nations Convention on the Law of the Sea to include provision for an international sea-bed authority to manage the mineral resources of the deep sea-bed for the benefit of all mankind. President Reagan cited these provisions as grounds for the refusal by the United States to sign the Convention.[33] It is not impossible to imagine how rivalry might develop over the exploitation of the ocean depths. If somebody discovers a submarine Klondike of sufficient richness, one nation may claim finder's rights; another maintain a geographical prerogative; signatories of the 1982 Convention demand a share; and the naval powers rely on their strength.

The third factor that could breed future conflict is the trend that some hoped would reduce its likelihood: what Ken Booth calls 'creeping jurisdiction'. He argues that progressive extension of national claims over the sea from 3 miles to 200 has already embraced 32 per cent of the oceans.[34] Even if the process goes no further – and there is no very obvious reason for supposing it has reached its final limit – the nations are already crowding one another at sea. It is not only between the Falkland Islands and the Argentinian mainland that the same strip of resource-bearing ocean is claimed by two naval powers. In the classical waters of the Aegean, Greek warships put to sea as often as Turkish research vessels are reported to be seeking oil-bearing strata.

In much of the animal kingdom the territorial instinct is considered a likely cause of conflict. Man is no exception – even at sea.

8 Piracy and Terrorism at Sea

With professed pirates there is no state of peace. They are the enemies of every country and at all times, and therefore are universally subject to the extreme rights of war. – LORD STOWELL[1]

Any illegal acts of violence, detention or any act of depredation, *committed for private ends* by the crew or the passengers of a *private ship* or a *private aircraft* . . . on the high seas . . . outside the jurisdiction of any state. – UN CONVENTION ON THE LAW OF THE SEA[2]

[It] would be a false characterization of illicit acts to describe them as piracy when the intention of the insurgents is to wage war. – O'CONNELL[3]

Anyone contemplating a voyage by sea may have good reason to prefer the vigorous view of the law stated in 1817 by Lord Stowell to the permissiveness recorded in 1984 by Professor O'Connell. There are today so many groups or gangs claiming political motives for the crimes they commit against inoffensive travellers that the exemption of insurgents from the penalties of piracy can only be deplored.

The rot set in with the 1958 Geneva Convention on the High Seas, which privatised piracy – against, be it noted, the opposition of the Soviet Union and their allies.[4] That doctrine was soon applied. On 23 January 1961 the Portuguese cruise liner SANTA MARIA was violently seized on the high seas by 71 Portuguese passengers led by a Captain Henrique Galvao. They claimed to be political insurgents against the Portuguese Government and thus not pirates, though their use of hand-grenades and machine-guns had killed one of the ship's officers and wounded eight of her crew. The Portuguese Government, however, thought they were pirates and asked the governments of Britain, the Netherlands and the United States, who had warships in the Caribbean, for assistance in their apprehension. The destroyer USS GEARING did intercept the SANTA MARIA, but, after discussions with Galvao, escorted the ship into the Brazilian port of Recife. There the passengers disembarked and the pirates (as even some Americans seem to have considered them) were granted asylum

92

before the ship returned to Portugal. This indulgence seems to have been prompted as much by political as by legal considerations. Technically the Geneva Convention of 1958 was not yet in force.[5]

A lesser incident occurred on 14 March 1970, when two armed sailors aboard the US cargo ship COLOMBIAN EAGLE seized control of the vessel and took her into a Cambodian port, where they asked for asylum, claiming to have acted in protest against the war in Vietnam. Twenty-four other members of the crew had previously been put into lifeboats. The ship was released on 8 April, having been followed into port by one of the ubiquitous cutters of the US Coast Guard.[6]

What might have become a more serious case was the capture of the Japanese ship SUEHIRO MARU in the Sulu Sea on 26 September 1975 by the Moro National Liberation Front. Threats were made against the crew and a ransom demanded, but negotiations secured the release of ship and crew.[7] The same gang captured the Malaysian vessel HALEHA BARU ADAL on 23 October 1979, killing and robbing some passengers and taking others hostage.[8]

These attacks were trifling by comparison with the vicious campaign of crime waged by mainly Thai pirates against the unfortunate Vietnamese who fled their own country in a variety of small craft. In the article quoted earlier P. W. Binnie suggests that during the period 1980–85 the number of Vietnamese killed was 1376, while 2283 women were raped and 522 kidnapped. According to *The Swiss Review of World Affairs* in January 1988:

> In the past two years an anti-piracy program, financed by Western countries and carried out by Thai naval and police units . . . seems to have had a certain deterrent effect, and the number of reported attacks on the boat people has declined sharply.

Five years seems a long time to wait for warships to get up enough steam to proceed against pirates. The countries of South East Asia all have navies and two of the world's strongest forces – the Soviet Pacific Fleet and the US Seventh Fleet – have nearby bases, at Cam Ranh Bay in Vietnam and at Subic Bay in the Philippines. In a strictly humanitarian role, some French and Italian warships have been reported as saving Vietnamese refugees whose boats were in danger of sinking and even more were taken on board passing merchant ships. The main organised rescue effort, however, seems to have come from two private organisations: the French Médecins du Monde and the German Cap Anamur Committee. These chartered special ships (partly financed by the television stations that put camera crews on board) to pick up refugees at sea. For some months in 1987 they were assisted by the French frigate BALNY and two auxiliaries, but the navies of the world have shown little eagerness to share in the task of suppressing piracy.[9]

If this inaction was prompted by the complacent assumption that only penniless refugees were at risk and that the recrudescence of piracy need not concern the naval powers, the error was soon exposed. Pirates boarded and robbed the tanker FALCON COUNTESS (chartered by the US Military Sealift Command) on 29 January 1985.

In February 1986 the Greek tanker MARIANNA and the Panamanian (Japanese-owned) freighter MONTE RUBY were among many merchant ships attacked by South East Asian pirates.[10] In May 1987 two Yugoslav, one Russian and one Norwegian ships suffered in the Singapore Straits. Nor is South East Asia the only danger zone: the west coast of Africa, Brazilian waters and the Caribbean have also experienced piratical attacks in the last decade. Estimates differ on the total number of ships that suffered, as they do on the definition of their misfortunes: anything between forty and eighty.

The controversy that nowadays surrounds acts of violence against ships at sea was strikingly apparent in the case of the ACHILLE LAURO. This Italian cruise liner was seized off the coast of Egypt on 7 October 1985 by four terrorists from the Palestine Liberation Front. Their stated purpose was to use those on board the liner as hostages for the release of fifty Palestinian prisoners in Israel. After murdering an elderly American passenger (presumably because he was a Jew) in his wheelchair, the terrorists appear to have lost their nerve, perhaps because there seemed to be no port to which they could safely take their prize: both Syria and Cyprus had rejected them. After a fruitless cruise the liner reversed her course and the terrorists entered into negotiations with Egyptian and Italian officials 15 miles off Port Said. These resulted in safe conduct for the terrorists, who were to be flown to Tunis (then the headquarters of the Palestine Liberation Organisation) in exchange for the release at Port Said of ship, crew and remaining passengers.

The United States Government was not a party to this deal. Regarding the terrorists as pirates it sent fighters from the carrier USS SARATOGA to intercept the Egyptian airliner on 10 October en route to Tunis and to force it to land at the NATO air base of Sigonella in Sicily. Here the terrorists were taken prisoner by the Italian police, the Italian Government having rejected the request made by the US Government that the prisoners should be transferred to American custody. With the exception of one Mahmoud Abul Abbas of the Palestine Liberation Organisation, who had acted as go-between in negotiations with the Egyptians and was allowed by the Italians to escape, the terrorists were charged and tried in an Italian court.

There was thus a conflict of legal views. The United States regarded the hijackers as pirates, *hostes humani generis* (enemies of the human race) whom any government might arrest on the high seas and whom any government could and should bring to justice for a universal crime. The United States even sent a detachment of their anti-terrorist Delta Force to Sigonella and it is said the Italians had to appeal to President Reagan to prevent their confrontation of the Italian police developing into actual conflict.

The Egyptian and Tunisian governments, on the other hand, seem to have considered the seizure of the ACHILLE LAURO as a political incident amenable to the usual political compromise. President Mubarak of Egypt was thus indignant at the forcing down of an Egyptian airliner, but went rather far when he described this action as 'piracy'. For the Italians it was an affair that had occurred aboard an Italian ship and one to be resolved as Italians thought fit. Unfortunately Italians evidently disagreed among themselves. In 1985 they allowed Abbas to escape to Belgrade (where the Yugoslavs refused, when asked by the Americans, to arrest him). The Italian Government resigned over the issue on 17 October, only to return to office on 8 November. Then, in 1986, an Italian court sentenced Abbas, in his absence, to life imprisonment. Nobody was entirely satisfied by the outcome.[11]

As these examples suggest, the problems created by piracy in the second half of the twentieth century tend to be political rather than naval. Although modern pirates have often profited by technological advances – using fast speedboats rather than junks in the South China Sea, for instance – the balance of advantage is on the other side. The ships – as opposed to the boats used by Vietnamese refugees – on which pirates prey can call for help by wireless, which can also coordinate the movements of warships. Aircraft can search widely for pirates, overtake and attack them. Warships have weapons of a range and power which pirates cannot match. If the eradication of piracy was the common purpose of the world's navies, the scourge could at least be reduced to the low level of the 1920s.

Naturally the situation is not as bad as it was in the eighteenth century. Then even the naval powers employed large numbers of privateers to prey upon the commerce of their enemies. These privateers were armed vessels owned and officered by private individuals, but given a commission (sometimes called a 'letter of marque') by a belligerent government to attack and plunder ships flying an enemy flag. Privateers operated at their own expense, but expected to profit by their licensed robbery. The governments that commissioned them escaped the cost of extra warships and the trouble as well as the expense of finding crews.

The superiority of private enterprise over nationalised industry might again have been demonstrated, but for one snag. Even in the eighteenth century war at sea was occasionally interrupted by intervals of peace. When this happened, not all the privateers had always made enough money to retire. Some of them just carried on – as pirates. Most governments disapproved, but – at least in seas as distant from major naval bases as the Caribbean – the factors that had encouraged the employment of privateers in time of war aggravated the difficulty of suppressing them in time of peace. Only after 1815, the year that ended the era of endemic naval war and established British naval supremacy, could the long task of eradicating piracy really begin. The Declaration of Paris, in 1856, that 'privateering is and remains abolished' symbolised one major advance. As the United States did not accede to this clause, President Jefferson Davis of the Confederate States decided to issue letters of marque to privateers during the American Civil War (1861–65).[12]

Progress against piracy – by the 1920s it had almost been confined to Chinese waters – nevertheless demanded a basic minimum of agreement among the naval powers that they had a common interest in the suppression of the practice. It is this political assumption which has been eroded in the second half of the twentieth century. The corrosive agent, where governments are concerned, is no longer the profit-motive, but ideological rivalry. Two centuries ago the difference between a privateer and a pirate was that between war and peace: a question of dates. What distinguishes today's pirate from a freedom fighter is only a point of view, an ideology.

In the late twentieth century a naval power may be reluctant, for political reasons, itself to undertake the suppression of piracy, or to cooperate with other naval powers in doing so or even to remain a passive spectator of the suppression of piracy. This reluctance often manifests itself in denial that the conduct complained of constitutes piracy at all. For instance, much of the argument concerning the definition of piracy in the 1958 Convention arose because Communist governments then wanted the seizure of merchant vessels by the warships of the Nationalist Chinese in Taiwan to be regarded as piracy. To the Americans, however, these actions were a legitimate exercise of belligerent rights by a recognised government.

This was not, of course, the attitude adopted by the government of the United States towards the depredations of the Confederate cruiser ALABAMA during the American Civil War. As for Confederate privateers, President Lincoln declared them to be pirates and was with difficulty dissuaded from ordering captured members of their crews to be hung.[13] Naturally, it is not only at sea that the moral flexibility characteristic of governments is manifested. Conduct which within the jurisdiction – of the Irish Republic, for instance – is treated as common crime easily undergoes political transfiguration across the frontier.

Civil wars present particular problems. Even third parties are often reluctant to concede full belligerent rights to the combatants. Nevertheless, the historical record does suggest that, if an organised group controls enough territory to have a capital and to call itself, with some degree of plausibility, a government, then the officers and men of any warship they commission have a good chance of escaping international condemnation as pirates.

Nor have the efforts made between the two world wars to stigmatise as piracy certain kinds of naval conflict – submarines sinking merchantmen without warning, for instance – proved lastingly viable. Indeed, they would probably have petered out well before the Second World War if Mussolini had been less reluctant to admit that that the 'unknown' submarines sinking merchant ships during the Spanish Civil War were actually Italian. After 1939 the world's naval officers discarded their kid gloves. Even when historians come to describe the Gulf War, they are unlikely to apply to Iranian tactics the words chosen by Ian Stewart, British Minister for the Armed Forces: 'controlled piracy.'[14] Merchant seamen sailing those waters in the 1980s may nevertheless be surprised to learn that history has reserved the epithet 'appeasers' for the British and French statesmen who decided, at Nyon in 1937, that 'warships which attacked neutral ships would be counter-attacked'.[15]

What does remain controversial is whether a non-governmental organisation administering no significant territory or population can organise violence against ships at sea without exposing its agents to treatment as pirates. Even if the 1982 United Nations Convention on the Law of the Sea is eventually revised to clarify this issue, the attitudes adopted by the naval powers in any given situation are more likely to be determined by what they see as their political interests than by legal judgements. It is the clash of conflicting interests and prejudices that has encouraged the revival of piracy in the second half of the twentieth century: that and the collapse of imperialism.

In this respect some forms of piracy belong in the same general category as the resistance movements of the Second World War, or the militant anti-colonialist organisations of the period that followed it, or the various terrorist organisations that now command some support among Basques, Irish Catholics, Palestinians, Tamils and others too numerous to list. They employ atrocious methods to promote a political cause that may or may not command a wider sympathy. Most of the governments that now deplore these practices have occasionally connived at them in the past – when some foreign gang seemed useful. Some governments still do.

Even when pirates do not profess political aims and seem to enjoy no government's backing, the present state of the world has alleviated the hostility of the environment in which they operate. In the South China Sea, for instance, the Super Powers are too preoccupied by their mutual rivalry to contemplate the distraction of a campaign against pirates, particularly as this might alienate those local governments which have themselves failed to take action – Thailand and the Philippines, for instance. Pirates can also take comfort from the fact that other forms of terrorism have so far commanded greater attention and excited more indignation.

It is true enough that far more terrorist activity occurs on land than at sea and that most people find it easier to identify themselves with the passengers of an airliner than with the crew of a cargo ship. It cannot be called surprising that the drastic action taken to apprehend the murderers of one American citizen aboard the ACHILLE LAURO was not even attempted in the case of the 1376 Vietnamese who perished at the hands of Thai pirates. Nevertheless future travellers may have bitter cause to regret this naval negligence.

If piracy at sea is still less prevalent than terrorism on land or in the air, little credit is due to the naval powers and none to their minimal readiness to cooperate in the eradication of this scourge. So far piracy has simply been less cost-effective. More men, weapons, equipment and experience are needed to board, let alone seize, a ship at sea. This is at best a relative deterrent and its importance is likely to decline. Other forms of terrorism occur within the jurisdiction of some state (even with aircraft the crunch usually comes when they have landed). Most states command greater resources than terrorist groups; many states are increasing this advantage by improving their precautions and the training of their special forces; the general trend, with due allowance for innovation, for surprise and for exceptional circumstances, is adverse to the further growth of successful terrorism on land. Pirates, however, can still hope to divide the nations and thereby enjoy the freedom of the seas.

For most of the 1960s and early 1970s a British frigate and detachments of Royal Marines were frequently required in the Bahamas to deter or repel incursions by groups of Cuban exiles opposed to the Castro Government in Havana. In September 1968, for instance, Marines from HMS ESKIMO captured a group of Cuban activists on South Andros. These Cubans could scarcely have made themselves such a nuisance so long if they had not enjoyed sympathy, support and even bases in the United States. Scholars have yet to identify the nation entitled to cast the first stone at those governments which support terrorism.

The motives of pirates are of secondary importance. If they are only intent on plunder or ransoms, their victims should theoretically stand a better chance of survival. In practice the Thai pirates have been as deadly as any political terrorist. Perhaps the political terrorist is more likely to find a safe haven and runs less risk that the major navies will join forces to seek and root him out. But ours is an age singularly inclined to condone any conduct that falls short of causing personal inconvenience to the rulers of nations.

A terrorist not preoccupied by the need to maximise the immediate booty of his followers may also be ready to attempt larger and more audacious enterprises. The mines that damaged 18 merchant ships in the Red Sea in July 1984 had supposedly been laid as an expression of Libyan indignation with Egypt.[16] Perhaps this should be regarded as a case of state terrorism, for it was not obviously lucrative. A pirate might not be able to extract much profit from capturing an oil tanker or a freighter laden with noxious chemicals. A terrorist might do so simply to be able to threaten pollution if his political demands were not met. Even destruction for its own sake – rather than as an instrument of extortion – may attract the true terrorist: blowing up an oil-rig, for instance. In 1975 the British response (which included the despatch of a warship) to a report (eventually revealed as false) that bombs had been planted on gas platforms off the Norfolk coast is said to have cost nearly half a million dollars. An actual explosion could easily have been 60 times more expensive.[17]

In the absence of something approaching a revolution in the conduct of international relations, pirates may reasonably expect to encounter less opposition than naval resources, above all than the coordinated use of naval resources, would permit. When piracy occurs (if international lawyers will forgive the solecism) in waters claimed as territorial, the pirate may only have to worry about the local navy, which he may be able to outrun or even to corrupt. In those parts of the high seas most favoured by pirates there is often no local navy able and willing to hunt them down, while the naval powers, if present at all, may cancel one another out.

Obviously there is a risk that piracy at sea will expand into this vacuum, but there are also signs that permissive trends in the maritime environment, long encouraged by contraction in British naval deployment, may be coming to an end. Of course, the US Navy, for ever preoccupied by the Russians, cannot be expected to match the exertions of the nineteenth-century Royal Navy, which faced no threat of sudden war and had no serious rival. Since 1983, however, when a single week saw pirates off Singapore attacking the American tanker SEALIFT ARCTIC and the freighter AMERICAN SPARTAN, action against pirates is believed to have figured in the training programme of the Naval Special Warfare Group at Coronado in San Diego Bay.[18] In 1984 the US Congress made provision for courts in the United States to try persons accused of taking Americans hostage, wherever the offence was committed.

That was what the US Government had wanted to arrange in the case of the ACHILLE LAURO and what they succeeded in doing in September 1987. Then one Fawaz Younis was lured aboard a boat operated by the Federal Bureau of Investigation and, once far enough into the Mediterranean, was arrested and transferred to the carrier USS SARATOGA in order to be flown to Washington and charged with hostage-taking in Beirut two years earlier. The US Attorney-General then promised that this would not be the last such operation.[19]

Punishment may sometimes be easier than prevention. As General Louis Menetrey, the United States Commander of Combined Forces in South Korea, commented when discussing the hazards to which the 1988 Olympic Games might be exposed in Seoul:

It would be difficult to stop, or to foreclose in advance, certain types of terrorism.

The General nevertheless meant to do what he could. One of the precautionary measures he revealed was the intended deployment in the region of an aircraft carrier battle-group, even though the presence of a similar force had not deterred a bomb outrage during the Asian Games of 1986 in Seoul. The role contemplated for the carrier was not explained: perhaps to maintain a combat air patrol over the stadium or to execute a retaliatory strike against Pyongyang?[20]

Governments with navies that are smaller and less widely deployed do not aspire to quite such far-reaching protection for their nationals, but even they must be ready to respond to some of the challenges posed by lawless violence at sea. Occasionally there is an element of ambiguity in their reaction. In October 1986, when the French fishery protection vessel ALBATROS chased and sank the Panamanian trawler SOUTHERN RAIDER in the Indian Ocean, the press suggested that the trawler had been mistaken for another vessel engaged in gunrunning. The trawler's crew, who survived, were only charged with illegal fishing.[21]

Mistakes can happen, but policing the oceans is a necessary task that is nowadays more often neglected than pursued with over-hasty zeal. As Brown, the great eighteenth-century landscape gardener, was fond of remarking, there is 'great capability of improvement here'. But the obstacles to be overcome, no less than the efforts required, are essentially political. Naval resources, to anyone but admirals intent on 'Der Tag', are ample whenever governments care to employ them.

9 Who Needs Ocean-going Navies?

> Our country has built a modern fleet and has sent it out into the ocean to ensure its state interests, in order to defend itself reliably from attack from extensive oceanic directions. – GORSHKOV[1]

> The United States is inevitably a maritime nation, and the United States and its Navy have inescapable global responsibilities. – WATKINS[2]

> Our long-term aim would be to confine the use of our armed forces outside the NATO area to disaster relief, participation in UN peacekeeping forces and similar roles . . . the practice of deploying naval task forces to 'show the flag' in the Pacific and Indian Oceans will cease. – BRITISH LABOUR PARTY[3]

One could comfortably fill a chapter with the contradictory pronouncements of the maritime nations concerning the role of their navies. Any appeal to manifest destiny is naturally nonsense. The Koreans displayed naval prowess – as they still do – centuries before either Americans or Russians had been heard of. Almost as long elapsed before any other Europeans emulated the global reach of the Vikings, still perhaps the most cost-effective sea predators human history knows. Naval ambitions and naval resources rise and fall not only with the balance of power in the world, but also with the variable chemistry of national politics.

There are two ways of trying to define an ocean-going navy: in terms of technical characteristics or of political and strategic functions. Most of the world's navies naturally fail both tests. All they can do and all they are meant to do is to provide a degree of coastal defence and to keep foreign fishing craft and other trespassers out of the exclusive economic zone. Only those nations with ambitions more extensive than mere estate management even consider the idea of an ocean-going navy and few of them have much chance of putting their idea into practice.

Technically one should not be too exacting. If a true ocean-going navy had to have integral air superiority, amphibious capability and full logistic support afloat, then only the United States Navy would qualify. And even they were revealed, in the summer of 1987, as lacking adequate minesweeping resources in the most active theatre of operations: the Persian Gulf. The true test of an ocean-going navy is its ability to sustain distant combat with a likely enemy. Readiness to fight anyone anywhere can be demanded only of a Super Power. Measuring the ocean-going effectiveness of lesser navies depends on an equation with many variables: distance, duration, the strength of the opponent, the type of operation needed, the political climate at home and abroad. No navy commands any absolute amount of power. What it can do varies from one conflict to another.

The Falklands War, for instance, tested the British navy to its ocean-going limit, not just in terms of distance, but in the combination of distance with other factors: the time to be spent at sea; the need for replenishment at sea; the ability to transport, land and provide air cover for troops as well as air defence for the fleet. Naturally risk is inseparable from such undertakings – 't'is not in mortals to command success' – but no great change in strategic parameters was needed to make this operation too hazardous to attempt: if the Royal Navy had been able to deploy only one aircraft carrier or if the operational radius of Argentine aircraft had been significantly greater.

If Operation Corporate represented about the most the Royal Navy, perhaps any navy other than those of the Super Powers, could be expected to achieve unaided, can one envisage a minimum qualification for ocean-going navies? Distance is perhaps the easiest test to set. An ocean-going navy must be capable of some kind of fighting, not merely beyond its 200-mile zone, but out of its own sea. There are navies, for instance in the Baltic and the Mediterranean, with no apparent plans or plausible capacities for remoter combat. The occasional cruise or visit, perhaps by a training ship, to some distant sea or port beyond the Straits or the Kattegat does not count.

The number and type of ships needed for a distant deployment will naturally vary. Different missions have very different require-ments, but distance alone is likely also to demand endurance – therefore reliefs, sea-going logistic support and a total strength in excess of the minimum needs of coastal defence. Six British warships, as well as auxiliaries, had to be committed in order to keep two in the Gulf.[4] Britain and France, as well as the Super Powers, have shown they can manage as much.

If West Germany or Italy wanted to deploy a larger force at such a distance, they might have to requisition extra logistic support – as even Britain did in 1982 – but both have some potential. In 1987

Italy sent some ships to the Persian Gulf and in October of that
year the Germans announced their intention of deploying to the
Mediterranean the destroyer MOELDERS and the frigate NIEDERSACHSEN
together with an auxiliary. The idea was to replace American warships
diverted to the Gulf.[5] China has exercised her warships at the other
end of the Pacific Ocean[6] and Japan could easily venture further
than, nowadays, she usually does. Australia has a small navy, but
has deployed ships quite far into the Indian and Pacific oceans. The
Indian Navy acquired a second aircraft carrier in 1987 and during
that year's disturbances in Ceylon there were Indian warships as far
south as Colombo. The navies of Argentina and Chile visit the
Antarctic, and Brazilian ships are frequent guests in West African
harbours.

Of course, it would be misleading to consider the ocean-going role
merely in the cold light of logistic reach, unfair to subject it to the
harsh tests of strategic realism. Distant seas lend enchantment to the
voices of those who must coax a naval budget from earthbound
bureaucrats. Admiral Merino, when interviewed for the journal
Naval Forces, was almost brutally frank about the limited resources
of the Chilean Navy he commanded. He even conceded that 'Chile
does not take part in global tasks.' The romantic strain he had striven
to repress nevertheless emerged in his declaration:

> our commitments go far beyond the 200-mile zone and include
> protection of national commercial routes and the Free World's sea
> lanes, which requires a blue water navy.

When it came to protecting the Chilean province of the Easter
Islands – 2000 miles from Valparaiso – the admiral was more cautious:

> . . . until the government has absorbed the costs which arose as a
> result of the 1985 earthquake.[7]

Officers in navies more lavishly endowed should not smile. Admiral
Merino was by no means the only naval visionary in the later 1980s
who clearly believed

> . . . a man's reach should exceed his grasp, Or what's a heaven
> for?'[8]

As far as resources go, these are the obvious naval candidates –
Super Powers apart – for the ocean-going certificate. There are others
who could manage it in conjunction with more sophisticated allies.
The Netherlands, for instance, sent minesweepers to the Persian Gulf

when promised British support in case of interference. Nine countries contribute ships to NATO's Standing Naval Force Atlantic. If the United Nations ever wanted to create an international task force for service in the Gulf or elsewhere, the least of their problems would be finding enough navies able to contribute an ocean-going ship or two. Success would depend on the political circumstances.

Resource constraints are often less critical than those imposed by political and strategic considerations. The Japanese Navy may be much smaller today than it was in 1941–42, when it set new standards for distant combat at sea, but it is the altered political climate in Japan that keeps the navy in home waters and restricts its task to close defence. The doctrine of non-alignment may one day be reinterpreted to allow the Indian Navy a more ambitious role in the Indian Ocean, but has hitherto been more of a check than a spur. Mutual rivalry keeps Greek and Turkish ships in the Mediterranean. Few countries are sufficiently confident of the security of their own coasts or have enough important interests beyond their regional sea to afford the luxury of an ocean-going navy.

If fully ocean-going navies are rarer today than they used to be – eight of them sent ships to protect the International Concession at Shanghai in 1927[9] – this is mainly due to the decline of imperialism. Navies and empires grew and flourished together, for colonies not only had to be acquired from, or defended against, distant enemies: they also provided the network of bases that so greatly reduced the extra cost of making a navy ocean-going. Even the United States became a major naval power only when, at the end of the nineteenth century, they seized some colonies from Spain. The nature of ocean-going navies was transformed when Japan, hitherto dominating only the adjacent Asian mainland, launched her campaign of conquest across the Pacific in 1941 and the United States, suddenly deprived of distant bases, had to create a new kind of navy that could do without them.

The greatly increased cost of giving a navy ocean-going capability was only one of the long-term results of the Pacific war. Another was the progressive liquidation of the empires that had provided such an important argument for having ocean-going navies. Of course, the Super Powers developed new, extensive and rival spheres of influence that had to be underpinned by navies of unprecedented power and sophistication. But, with every colony that withered from the imperial vine, the residual requirements of old empires seemed more of a pretext and less of a reason for Britain and France to keep ocean-going navies. Those colonies that remained – often more of a liability than an asset – had insufficient glamour to dispel the heresy that (more in Britain than in France) originated on the Left and, until 1982, was spreading to the Right: distant conflict was best avoided by dispensing with the kind of navy that could fight it.

OCEAN-GOING NAVIES FOR SUPER POWERS

That is not a doctrine likely to commend itself to either Super Power. Perhaps the expansion into the oceans of the Soviet Navy during the second half of the twentieth century was less predictable than that of the United States Navy during the first half. It may not even have been inevitable. But it happened and the Russians cannot now be expected to withdraw before the Americans agree to do the same. Whether that could ever occur is a question to be considered in the next chapter.

By 1987, when both Super Powers were showing signs of economic strain, they had significantly increased the ocean-going capability of their navies. 'The surface forces of the Soviet Navy', in the words of their principal rival,

> continue to improve their ability to fulfill a broad range of naval operations, especially in waters distant from the USSR . . . the trend . . . has been toward larger units with more sophisticated weapons and sensors. These ships can cruise for longer distances, carry more ordnance, and conduct a greater range of operations than their predecessors. This development has created a new flexibility for Soviet surface forces in carrying out deployed operations on a worldwide scale.[10]

The main American reservation is that

> Sustained combat operations in Third World areas, however, would require underway replenishment ship support of a kind that the Soviets currently lack.[11]

As for the US Navy, the Americans claim that

> Over the past 6 years, impressive progress has been made in restoring the maritime strength required to maintain our global defense responsibilities. . . . All our naval improvements bolster deterrence by showing our adversary that he cannot control the sea, nor prevent our maritime support of US forces and interests worldwide.[12]

Over a thousand ships, to say nothing of aircraft, auxiliaries, bases, communication satellites, manoeuvres, reconnaissance of various kinds and treaties with dubious clients, testify to the extreme importance attached by the Super Powers to the possession of ocean-going navies. War between the Super Powers is probably regarded, in both countries, as the ultimate justification for all this effort and expenditure. American admirals hasten to add that war is a contingency they seek to deter; their rivals see aggression against the Soviet Union as the only possible cause. If war at this level has not yet happened, it remains a possibility. Whether anyone could win or survive it is uncertain, but it is naturally open to admirals to argue that the chances would be even worse without a navy than with one.

Earlier arguments concerning naval war, total or limited, past or future, need not be repeated here. Even in violent peace Super Powers need ocean-going navies, because each claims a global role and is convinced of the other's hostility. President Reagan meant what he said when he told Vice-Admiral Kelsow, who commanded the Sixth Fleet during the March 1986 attack on Libya:

> you have sent a message to *the whole world* that the United States has the will and, through you, the ability to defend the free world's interests.[13]

So did President Gromyko, his words enshrined in the official history of Soviet foreign policy:

> Today no problem of international importance, no fundamental issue facing the modern world, can be decided without the communist movement, and particularly without its integral component – the ruling parties of the countries of the socialist community.[14]

In the furtherance of such ambitions an ocean-going navy could usefully supplement American money and Russian ideology. The tighter the money gets and the more tarnished the ideology, the greater the relative importance of navies is likely to become. The purposes for which the Super Powers use their ships will not always be welcome to third parties, but no navy has yet done as much damage – to its victims or its owner – as have armies and air forces. As long as it is only violent peace, co-existence should be possible – for ocean-going navies and the human race.

AND FOR THE REST

Britain and France, at present the two other countries with undeniably ocean-going navies, are not in the same league nor subject to similar compulsions of rivalry for the primacy of power. Their navies are not only much smaller, but also less sophisticated than those of the Super Powers. Their cost has nevertheless proved a burden which Japan and Germany – richer countries that were once major naval powers – have preferred to avoid. The German preference is understandable. Their eastern boundary is potentially the world's most demanding front line. They also have less need of the sea than the French. But the Japanese, in their islands, must import, over greater oceanic distances, even more of their energy and raw materials than the British. They have accordingly increased their merchant and fishing fleets and maintained their shipbuilding capacity, while the British have allowed theirs to go into free fall. If naval strength were a function of economic needs and economic resources, Japan's would not merely surpass that of Britain and France: it would rival the fleets of the Super Powers.

As usual it is politics that is in command, not merely in the special case of late twentieth-century Japan, but also in Britain and France. Those two nations have been accustomed over the centuries to leading roles on the international stage. Even in relatively reduced circumstances they have not managed too badly: permanent members of the Security Council of the United Nations, for instance, when larger, richer or more populous countries must queue and lobby for their turn. Ocean-going navies, no less than nuclear weapons or unusually widespread and expensive diplomatic representation, are a contribution to the cost of a first-class ticket. They help to maintain the appearance of a global presence.

France, with no ships committed to NATO and correspondingly fewer doctrinal inhibitions, can go further in this direction than Britain, regularly maintaining small forces in both the Indian and the Pacific oceans. '. . . the French Navy manoeuvres to display its support and loyalty to treaty partners, allies and former colonies.'[15] An Indian admiral took a less friendly view.

Neither Holland nor Britain now maintains a demonstrable naval presence in the Indian Ocean. France stations warships in it, using facilities at Djibouti (Somalia) and Réunion Island. This is supposed to notify her resolve to protect her maritime interests in the area, but countries with fresh memories of events in Algeria and Vietnam scent the stale whiff of a colonial hangover in it.[16]

Manoeuvres are necessary. What might happen in general war receives an extra veil from the misty ambiguity of French policy towards the North Atlantic Alliance. Nevertheless, the French Navy is quite as capable of an ocean-going role as the British, in spite of the latter's more elaborate network of plans, commands and commitments. Why the French need such a role is sometimes less clear. Apologists for French naval policy tend to rely on abstract concepts: security of access to overseas territories or friendly countries; continuous manifestation of a maritime presence. There is an understandable reluctance to indicate any kind of scenario or to specify the political requirement for overseas presence in peace or distant combat in war.

The French are not alone in their reticence, but Admiral Hill's comparison of French with British practice is instructive.

There is a distinction, though it can be overdone, between permanent and intermittent maritime presence. In general, the French pattern in recent years has been to maintain rather low-capability forces permanently in such areas as Djibouti and the southern Indian Ocean, while the British have deployed balanced forces of several powerful warships about once a year on peripatetic tours of the Indian Ocean and Far East. The French system has the advantage of permanence, of clear readiness; but it may be the permanence of weakness, an invitation to pre-emption. The British system is more overtly a flag-showing parade, demonstrating ready power, and it has the advantage of being capable while in an area of significant impact in a variety of ways from children's parties through flood relief to deterrent effects; but when it is not there it isn't, and out of sight may be out of mind.[17]

The Persian Gulf, where outside navies encounter a situation that is – for them – neither war nor peace, has provided a partial exception to these and other rules. It has attracted ships usually reluctant to leave their own seas – from the navies of Belgium, Italy and the Netherlands. In 1987 France conspicuously increased her presence, Britain more modestly. It was in November 1986, however, that the Royal Navy sent a distinctly stronger force – the carrier ILLUSTRIOUS, the assault ship INTREPID, the destroyer NOTTINGHAM and the frigate ANDROMEDA, with three auxiliaries – not to the Persian Gulf, but to the Arabian Sea: not for operations, but for an exercise with army and air force units, as well as Omani forces.[18] Neither this exercise nor the earlier RIMPAC (in the Pacific with the Australian, Canadian, Japanese and US navies)[19] took place in waters where British ships could be expected to fight, least of all in general war.

Naturally no one knows whether general war, if it ever comes, will last long enough to offer much scope for any warships but strategic submarines – those ultimate symbols of the death wish. The scenarios in which the British and French navies help to preserve the existence of their nations by giving useful assistance to the United States Navy are a credit to the imagination of the naval officers who devised them. As contingencies they deserve inclusion in a category even more important at sea than elsewhere: the unforeseen. Nevertheless, if they are to survive interested attack from generals and air marshals, to say nothing of the ingrained hostility of finance ministers and their advisers, any practical conclusions they are intended to support do need some reinforcement.

For the Europeans, to some extent also for the Super Powers, ideas of future war tend to be dominated by the prospect of fighting on the Central Front. Even today that assumption may not be wholly valid and it is easy to imagine ways in which it might be eroded. The Pacific Basin is becoming more important to the Super Powers, the cleavage between East and West in Europe less acute. The time may come when Germany is no longer seen as the obvious battleground, when the rival alliances will agree to withdraw the foreign armies and air forces stationed in that country. At present – and no early change is yet foreseeable – the conventional wisdom expects the course of fighting on the Central Front to decide whether general war will be short or long, conventional or nuclear, winnable or not. The scenarios in vogue have mostly been devised by soldiers and airmen. Few of them envisage a major role for navies and those that do, assume that 'political warning-time' will permit seaborne reinforcement or forward deployment before fighting even begins on land.

Such notions do not detract from the global role of the United States Navy. They do not greatly disturb French semi-detachment. It is in Britain that admirals need to beware of the single, Central Front scenario. Some of its variants have little use for ocean-going surface warships. If the fleet is to be preserved in the face of fierce competition for scarce resources, it will not merely be necessary to elaborate alternative hypotheses: contributing to the Maritime Strategy, for instance, or bolstering the Northern Flank. This is pitting one guess against another. More telling arguments will be needed to resist a renewal of the 1981 attack on a navy obstinately maintaining 'large numbers of every type of platform.'[20]

The best reason for having an ocean-going navy has always been the extra chance it offers of responding to the unforeseen, but ocean-going navies are also needed by governments seeking a wider role in world affairs than their own region affords. They are not purely defensive forces. Even for islands, even for Super Powers, it is no longer as true as it was in Bacon's day that 'he that commands the sea is at great liberty, and may take as much and as little of the war as he will'. What ocean-going navies do offer, apart from a seaborne nuclear deterrent and the hypothetical opportunities of conceivable kinds of general war, is the chance of distant intervention.

That may be intended to frustrate a rival or to assist a friend. It may be in limited war or in one of the many gradations of gunboat diplomacy; by showing the flag or by rescuing those in peril. The purpose may be honest or sinister, well or ill conceived and executed. Ocean-going warships provide governments with an extra tool, a set of lazy tongs, an extended reach. Their utility is likely to last as long as violent peace, but nations with no desire to stick their necks out may prefer to shorten their vision and keep their navies at home.

10 Arms Control at Sea

> [Great] armaments lead inevitably to war. – GREY OF FALLODON[1]

> [Warships] can provoke trouble, shape the will to use them and provide options which are better left uncontemplated . . . , without surface warships the British government could hardly have contemplated the retaking of the Falkland Islands in 1982. – KEN BOOTH[2]

> [The] development of naval capabilities . . . has, in the geopolitical circumstances since 1945, become a competitive accumulation and qualitative refinement of arms with a momentum of its own . . . the naval arms race. – UN STUDY, 1985[3]

> Bad workmen blame their tools – PROVERB

Earlier chapters have provided various instances of an obvious truth: navies can be foolishly employed as well as wisely, for bad ends as easily as for good. It is not even true that political leaders, who should be the ultimate masters, are always and alone to blame. A navy is not a machine, idling in neutral and passively awaiting orders. Tirpitz, Fisher, Yonai, Darlan, Radford, Gorshkov were admirals as much concerned with policy as with its execution. They influenced, as have other admirals still alive, the choice of national objectives. The existence of a navy, particularly an ocean-going navy, may not only provide a government with additional options, but constitute a less than silent reproach of any failure to exploit them. Warships can provoke as well as protect and prevent.

Navies are not unique in being instruments of power able, under conscious direction, to serve different purposes. During the twentieth century, motor vehicles have increasingly transformed the everyday existence of many nations. They have conferred great benefits, caused gross pollution and, since 1945, killed and injured far more people than all the navies of the world. Their abolition is an idea that commands no serious support, but strenuous efforts have long been made, with only limited success, to control their use.

The control of navies encounters even greater obstacles. All warships embody the principle of hostility which only some drivers impart to their vehicles. The states that own warships are divided among themselves by conflicts of interest, by prejudice and by mutual fear. There is no international authority able to license warships or to prescribe, let alone enforce, any rules of conduct for their drivers. The few measures of control agreed among particular states represent a compromise, usually an unsatisfactory compromise, between the desire to inflict injury and the fear of suffering it. Such compromises must be negotiated piecemeal, are seldom widely applicable and have usually proved ephemeral. During the twentieth century, agreement has occasionally been reached or proposed to restrict the size of navies and their armament; their deployment; or their conduct in time of peace.

SIZE AND ARMAMENT

In the past this has usually been reckoned the most significant aspect of naval arms control. In 1912, for instance, when Britain and Germany had for years been competitively building battleships, Winston Churchill, then First Lord of the Admiralty, offered to cancel the five British battleships projected for 1913 if Germany would abandon her three.[4] This was the characteristic British attitude in the years before the First World War: priority for reciprocal limitations in naval strength, particularly in battleships. Lloyd George, then Chancellor of the Exchequer and personally opposed to any increase in naval strength, told the German Ambassador in 1908, as the latter reported:

> a slowing down of the tempo in our fleet-building would contribute more quickly to reassure public opinion, than any political action could.

Kaiser Wilhelm II described this as an 'unheard-of demand' and endorsed the Ambassador's argument:

> as long as the English defence policy tended to create uneasiness in Germany, I considered a curtailment in the armaments at sea as being out of the question.[5]

It would be a serious over-simplification to say that Britain regarded the High Seas Fleet as the only obstacle to friendship with Germany and that the Germans considered the High Seas Fleet the necessary response to British hostility, but these were the debating positions favoured on either side of the North Sea. It can also be said that Germany wanted a political price – a free hand in Europe – for any naval concession, that was higher than Britain was prepared to pay.

One of the results of the First World War was the elimination of the High Seas Fleet (scuttled while interned at the British base of Scapa Flow), but the United States, as greatly enriched by the war as Britain was impoverished, now emerged as a new naval challenger. President Harding, however, unlike his admirals, favoured disarmament, and the Washington Treaty of 1922 produced actual naval reductions on a scale never approached before or since. Britain scrapped 24 capital ships, the United States (counting those under construction) 26 and Japan 16. Britain, the United States, Japan, France and Italy (by then the only significant naval powers) also accepted a range of restrictions on the future numbers, size and armament of their capital ships, aircraft carriers and cruisers. Until Japan denounced it in 1934 the Treaty had been reasonably well observed by its signatories, but it lapsed in 1936.

Other naval agreements during the 1930s were less comprehensive and resulted in much smaller reductions, sometimes only in agreement to restrict new construction. In 1935 the Anglo-German Naval Agreement even extended a British blessing to the (probably inevitable) rebuilding of the German Navy. It has sometimes been argued that this era of naval disarmament, which lacked any substantial counterpart in political agreement, did more harm than good to the prospects for peace.

Nevertheless the interwar period was noteworthy, as earlier and later decades were not, for significant multilateral reductions in naval strength. To a considerable extent this was a straightforward reaction to what were then considered the mistakes made before 1914. It is also true that the technical problems of naval disarmament were simpler in the first half of the twentieth century than they have been in the second. Before 1914, to some extent even before 1939, there was more equivalence between one warship and another of the same class. British and German battleships might differ in speed, armament and protection – even inside the two navies – but these differences evened themselves out in a fleet where all had to move at the same speed and operate at the same range. Purely numerical comparisons have become progressively more difficult ever since. If the leading naval powers wanted, in the last decade of the century, to make equal reductions in their navies, they would encounter complex and controversial problems in drawing up an agreed list of ships.

Perhaps this is one of the reasons why recent attempts at naval arms control have focused almost exclusively on certain types of nuclear weapon. In essence they have been offshoots from wider negotiations on the general issue of strategic arms, whether land-based, airborne or submarine-launched. The Strategic Arms Limitation Treaty of 1972 (SALT II), for instance, restricted the number of ballistic missile launchers in submarines. No similar constraints have been agreed for other kinds of warships or naval weapons. They have not even been proposed. *Strategic Survey*, the annual publication by the International Institute for Strategic Studies, has had a section on the progress of arms control negotiations in every year from 1977 to 1986. Except for missiles (ballistic and cruise) carrying nuclear weapons, there has never been a suggestion that the naval powers might reduce the number or the capabilities of their ships.

So far nuclear weapons on land have seemed more amenable to arms control than those at sea. Many of the larger land-based missiles can be identified and counted from satellites in space. The mobile variety do not move fast or far enough to be easily hidden. At sea the problem is more complicated. Submarines can be counted, even if they cannot be reliably located, and the number of their missiles calculated. These are assumed, even admitted, to have nuclear warheads. But what about other warships? It is harder to ascertain whether or not the missiles they carry are, or can be, fitted with nuclear warheads. The United States sacrificed an ally rather than answer that question. And the nominal range of those missiles is almost irrelevant. Ships, unlike silos or the monstrous vehicles that lumber out from Greenham Common, can move thousands of miles. The nuclear-armed variety of the American sea-launched cruise missile Tomahawk is said to have a range of 1500 miles. US warships are frequent visitors to the wide expanses of ocean waste within that distance of the Kola bases, of Vladivostok, of Petropavlovsk.

It is scarcely surprising to read that:

US acceptance of an arms control agreement affecting cruise missiles [Gorbachev in 1986 had proposed their elimination from surface warships and limits on their submarine deployment][6] appears improbable for a number of reasons. The virtual impossibility of distinguishing between nuclear and conventional warheads when deployed on board ships . . . would require unique and intrusive verification measures . . . any ban . . . would likely bar use of conventional variants . . . a complete ban on the weapon . . . would not avoid the inevitable prospect that other countries would acquire and field cruise missiles.[7]

The final argument may seem a trifle strained – 'The Soviet Union has deployed nuclear-armed cruise missiles at sea since 1962'[8] – and even in the United States Tomahawk is a controversial weapon, but the years of debate on this issue tend to support the view that, at sea, most weapons will be harder to limit than the ships or submarines that carry them. In June 1985, for instance, President Reagan announced that the United States, in order to remain within the limits fixed by the SALT II Treaty, would dismantle not the excess Poseidon missiles, but the submarine that housed them.[9] Yet no agreement has been reached for over half a century actually to reduce the number of surface warships.

For this the altered political perspective of our times is partly to blame. The conventional wisdom of one era is often a reaction against what are seen as the major errors of earlier years. In the 1920s and the first half of the 1930s, for instance, the 1914–18 war was widely (not universally) regarded as a disastrous and wholly unnecessary conflict among European nations with compatible social structures and systems of government. As the war could not be explained by the clash of rival ideologies or as a rational quest for material advantage, it was natural enough to consider it the unintended result of an arms race spiralling out of control.

This view was even reinforced by the coincidence that Germany, the main loser in the First World War, had also been the principal opponent of any kind of disarmament, not only in pre-1914 naval discussions with Britain, but also in the international conferences of 1899 and 1907 at the Hague.

The Second World War, however, was arguably ideological in origin and might even have been precipitated by the partial disarmament of those countries most anxious to preserve the peace. When it was over and a shell-shocked generation were then confronted, in the late 1940s, by a different but equally challenging ideological rivalry, the lesson they thought they had learned was that peace could only be preserved by preparing for war. Although disarmament was occasionally advocated, actual reductions were usually unilateral and prompted by economic stringency. As the United Nations Study Group said in 1985, 'naval arms limitations have received almost no attention in recent years'.[10]

It remains to be seen whether the United States and the Soviet Union will honour their agreement to scrap a small percentage of the nuclear weapons they now deploy; whether they will refrain from compensating measures and whether the net result will amount to a significant reduction. The prospects for other forms of actual disarmament are not at present promising, least of all at sea, until there has been a major improvement in the political climate.

RESTRICTIONS ON DEPLOYMENT

Throughout the twentieth century there have been sporadic attempts at quite a different kind of arms control at sea. Instead of trying to limit the strength of navies, whether in terms of ships or of their armament, the objective has been to constrain their movements in time of peace. The risks of conflict between naval powers could, it was argued, be reduced if their warships avoided confrontation at sea or unwelcome approaches to one another's coasts. This geographical approach to arms control often included undertakings that particular islands or straits would not be fortified or employed as naval bases.

One of the oldest issues in the geographical branch of naval arms control concerns the Straits joining the Black and Mediterranean seas: the Bosphorous and the Dardanelles. Throughout the nineteenth and twentieth centuries successive international agreements contained different definitions (they varied with the fortunes of the most recent war and with the balance of power in any given era) of the rights of the various states concerned. From the Russian standpoint the ideal arrangement was that of the Treaty of Unkiar Skelessi in 1833: their warships were allowed free egress from the Black Sea, but those of other nations were not allowed in. The opposite extreme was reached in 1856, when Russia (who had just lost the Crimean War) was forbidden to maintain any armed forces in the Black Sea. Everything in between has been tried, but the present compromise derives from the surprisingly long-lived Montreux Convention of 1936.

This imposed various restrictions on the number and type of non-Turkish warships allowed through the Straits in peacetime and required prior notice of their passage to be given to the Turkish authorities. The survival of the Convention is due to Turkish toughness in 1945, when even the United States were ready to see the Convention amended to suit the Soviet Union, but also to subsequent Turkish flexibility in its detailed interpretation.

Aircraft carriers, for instance, are not included among the warships specified in the Convention as eligible to pass the Straits. Indeed, Litvinov, the Soviet delegate at Montreux, had originally proposed that the passage of aircraft carriers (of which the Soviet Union then had none) should be specifically prohibited.[11] When MOSKVA sallied out in 1968, later followed by LENINGRAD and, in 1976, by KIEV, the Turkish Government accepted the Soviet description of these ships as 'anti-submarine cruisers'.[12]

Both the Soviet Union and Turkey had a case. The Convention was not very tightly drafted and the Russians were not alone in their invention of new names for carriers. In the 1970s the British, for reasons of domestic rather than international politics, called the Invincible-class 'through-deck cruisers'. In 1979 the Ministry of Defence even adopted the Russian name 'anti-submarine cruiser'.[13] Moreover, as early as 1956, the declared aircraft carrier HMS EAGLE made an almost complete passage of the Bosphorous *after* a visit to Istanbul (traversing the Dardanelles on a courtesy visit at the invitation of the Turkish Government was allowed by the Convention).[14] For one reason or another, the passage of KIEV (nowadays called by the Russians an 'aircraft-carrying cruiser') and, in 1979, of her sister ship MINSK, attracted no formal protest.

Otherwise the Convention has, on the whole, been observed. Soviet submarines in the Mediterranean come from the Northern and Baltic Fleets and advance notice is given of the movement of surface ships to and from the Black Sea Fleet. The survival of the Convention is obviously convenient to Turkey, giving her some control over the use by foreign warships of what might otherwise be an international strait. Each of the naval powers has cause to deplore some provision of the Convention, but it is arguable that any regulation of such contentious issues is better than none at all. If international friction has not been eliminated – the annual incursions into the Black Sea of the US Navy are permitted by the Convention – it can easily be argued that the results of abolition would be worse and that no better alternative is likely to be negotiable.

What makes regulating the use of the Turkish Straits such a chronic problem is that it has always been an attempt to treat the symptoms rather than the cause of dispute. What is mainly at issue nowadays is naval ascendancy in the Mediterranean. Since 1946, when the US Government announced that their warships would be permanently stationed in the Mediterranean to carry out American policy and diplomacy, the US Navy has provided the resident champion – long before the Soviet Navy was ready to renew the challenge posed by its Tsarist predecessor to the British. Moreover, these American ships devote most of their peacetime efforts to objectives not directly related to the Soviet Mediterranean Squadron: defying Libya, encouraging Egypt or Jordan, reinforcing Israel.

It is unlikely, therefore, that Gorbachev expected much American response to his proposal of 26 March 1986:

> If the United States, which is situated thousands upon thousands of miles away from the Mediterranean, pulled its fleet out of there, the Soviet Union would simultaneously do the same. We are prepared without delay to enter talks on the issue.

Two years later he even lowered his sights, suggesting only that the Super Powers should 'freeze' the number of their ships in the Mediterranean. No butter melted in the mouth that uttered the cool response:

> a freeze, as suggested by Mr Gorbachev, would interfere with the free movement of innocent warships on the high seas.[15]

On the other side of the globe, in July 1986, he may only have been teasing when he hinted at Soviet readiness to abandon their base at Cam Ranh Bay if the US Navy left the Philippines, but the suggestion opens up an intriguing vista for political speculation. American leases on their two bases in the Philippines are due for review in 1988. Local hostility to the American presence has been growing and renewal of the arrangement cannot be taken for granted. Naturally the hostility expressed in March 1988 by the Philippine Foreign Secretary, Raul Manglapus, who said the bases were 'obviously an irritant', may have been partly a bargaining gambit. Nevertheless the impoverished Philippine Government, whose hold on power is precarious, may want more money than the Americans care to pay or may wish to subject American use of the bases to vexatious conditions.

The second half of the twentieth century has not been an era particularly congenial to the maintenance of military or naval bases in populated foreign territory. In 1987 the United States were engaged in difficult negotiations over their bases in Spain and Greece. If the outcome of that year's British elections had been different, the Americans might have had even more trouble in that country. In Turkey and Portugal American prospects are still a little uncertain. When considering the outlook in the Philippines, it is worth recalling that in earlier years as many as nine countries had refused to extend American base agreements.[16] Will the Russians remember to withdraw their offer before the Americans want to accept it?

So far, of course, such Soviet proposals have been virtually risk-free. Gorbachev's suggestion of 27 November 1986 for 'substantially reducing the size of naval forces in the Indian Ocean'[17] had earlier been heard from Brezhnev. Admittedly the idea of a zone of peace in the Indian Ocean had actually been discussed with the United States Government during the Carter presidency, but, doubtless to the relief of admirals in Moscow as well as those in Washington, the talks ended abruptly after Soviet intervention in Afghanistan.

Nevertheless, international agreement to constrain naval deployment has long been the objective of Soviet diplomacy. On 15 April 1984 Gromyko, then Soviet Foreign Minister, addressed a letter to the Secretary-General of the United Nations[18] suggesting negotiations aimed at the curtailment of naval activity in areas of tension, of long-term deployment in distant seas and of the carriage of naval nuclear weapons in certain areas. Principles of this kind have often been endorsed by non-aligned countries in Latin America or around the shores of the Mediterranean. From 1971 the General Assembly of the United Nations have repeatedly declared the Indian Ocean to be a 'zone of peace' and similar ideas have been mooted by nations in South East Asia and the South Pacific. Various nations without nuclear weapons have subscribed to treaties and declarations prohibiting the presence of such weapons in certain oceans. Their wishes have not always been respected by those states whose ships carry such weapons.

Not all these ideas have been explored in sufficient detail – nor all these treaties widely enough negotiated – to expose them to the tests sensibly suggested by the United Nations Study on the Naval Arms Race.

A key ingredient of any limitation measure, and of its subsequent success and longevity, rests in the fact that it must contain something of great value to each and every signatory. Without this ingredient, a State may consider that the gain to be had from the proposed agreement is not worth the concessions that have to be made. Furthermore, progress in such negotiations cannot proceed in a political vacuum but is subject to the general pressures and climate of international relations between States.[19]

A major obstacle is implicit in the declaration made in January 1986, already quoted, by Admiral James D. Watkins USN:

The United States is inevitably a maritime nation, and the United States and its Navy have inescapable global responsibilities.[20]

Their allies, particularly the British, who took that line as long as they could afford to, may well be willing to endorse this formulation of Orwell's great axiom:

All animals are equal, but some animals are more equal than others.[21]

What is obvious is that the geographical approach to arms limitation cannot be halted at high-water mark. The example of the Antarctic Treaty of 1959, which prohibited all military activity, by land or sea, below 60° south latitude, may not lend itself to general imitation elsewhere, but it remains the ideal.

When Gorbachev made his speech of 1 October 1987 at Murmansk, he began with a passage of striking rhetoric:

In the North of the Earth, the Arctic, as in perhaps no other place . . . one can clearly feel – the chilling breath of the Pentagon's polar strategy: a gigantic potential of nuclear destruction is concentrated on submarines and surface ships.

When he went on to 'propose examination of banning naval activity in mutually agreed zones of international straits and on intensive shipping lanes altogether', one wonders how seriously he expected even Soviet naval officers to regard his words as the basis for a negotiable agenda. They were imaginatively chosen, but the long extract from his speech published in *Naval Forces* No. VI/1987 is not rich in that ingredient declared by the United Nations Study Group to be indispensable: 'something of great value to each and every' potential participant in the conference he suggested should be held at Leningrad.

This *quid pro quo* is needed even if the proposals are less ambitious and more precise. If outside navies are to be excluded from, for instance, the Mediterranean, then the states bordering that sea must be given sufficient cause for confidence in their own security to relinquish any thought of ever needing seaborne assistance. And that is only the first step. A naval power renouncing the right of peacetime access (no promise holds good in war) will naturally expect some compensation. The reciprocal withdrawal of another navy may not be enough to preserve the balance of power. Political disputes need to be settled – at least to be compromised – before adversaries can be expected to lay aside their weapons.

NAVAL CONDUCT IN TIME OF PEACE

Because men of war have always been liable to run across one another, fully armed, in the neutral wastes of the high seas, their conduct in time of peace has to be punctilious. This may have been easier when the officers of the world's navies were more conscious of their common status and mutual obligations as gentlemen. Lord Chatfield, who had been First Sea Lord during many tense encounters off the coast of a Spain racked by civil war, recalled that 'extreme courtesy existed between the Spanish and British sailors, almost as in the days of Nelson.' This courtesy may have been superficial, but no such comment could have been expected, in recent years, from the Mediterranean or the Persian Gulf.[22]

Nowadays the elementary rules of good manners have to be laboriously negotiated and then specified in international treaties that are not always observed. In 1972 the *American–Soviet Agreement on the Prevention of Incidents on and over the High Seas* spelled out what naval officers had for centuries taken for granted:

> no attacks to be simulated nor any objects launched, in the vicinity of the other party's ships.[23]

This provision again appeared in the *Soviet–British Incidents at Sea Agreement* of 1986 (Article III):

> Ships of the Parties shall not simulate attacks by aiming guns, missile launchers, torpedo tubes and other weapons in the direction of passing ships of the other Party.[24]

Once upon a time this obligation was taken so much for granted that in 1893, when a French cruiser turned her guns towards a British cruiser, Kaiser Wilhelm II, then visiting Queen Victoria, could envisage no option but war. Fortunately the French Admiral, too shocked at this behaviour even to await a protest, sent the offending captain to apologise for this 'unprovoked breach of correct naval conduct'.[25] In 1937 even Chatfield thought Admiral Ramsey had gone too far in his spontaneous apology to the captain of the Spanish cruiser ALMIRANTE CERVERA for the conduct of the British battleship RESOLUTION,[26] but the high priority accorded to international courtesy by naval officers was then obvious.

In October 1973, the year after the American–Soviet Agreement, the Soviets began large-scale anticarrier exercises against this carrier group with cruise-missile submarine participation. These exercises – the Soviet Navy's equivalent of training its guns on the US fleet – continued until November 3.[27]

This confrontation in the Mediterranean occurred at the height of the most acute Super Power crisis since Cuba in 1962.

What is more surprising is that the American author describing this sustained demonstration of hostility could nevertheless write, in the same chapter:

> the likelihood of such incidents [an encounter that occurred in 1970] has been reduced significantly by the adherence of the US and the USSR to the Incidents at Sea Agreement of 1972. Agreements of this sort appear to be a particularly desirable way to reduce the risk inherent in circumstances where the close and nearly constant interactions between the two navies in a crisis atmosphere can give rise to potentially incendiary situations.[28]

It is certainly arguable that the general incidence of dangerous discourtesy at sea has been reduced by the 1972 Agreement, but it is not reassuring that the agreement failed its first and, so far, its sharpest test. It is also a trifle disconcerting to read, in a Special Report by the American Institute for Foreign Policy Analysis, an article by Norman Friedman arguing for more permissive rules of engagement – 'the standing orders which govern a commander's ability to open fire' – which makes no reference to the fifteen-year-old American–Soviet Agreement.[29]

Analogous proposals in the general category known as 'confidence-building measures' have been discussed in the United Nations Disarmament Commission, the Stockholm Conference on Confidence-and-Security-Building Measures in Europe and the US–Soviet Nuclear and Space Arms Talks at Geneva. Little sea-related progress has been made. Soviet proposals have tended to be rather broad-brush, mixing conduct at sea with geographical constraints and even arms reductions. American reactions have often been suspicious:

> To constrain naval forces in the name of building confidence begs a key question: confidence on whose part? . . . the selection of naval forces does not appear to favour the West.[30]

Without some improvement in the general climate of international relations it may even be premature to expect sailors to catch up with soldiers. In Europe, for instance, 42 days' notice must nowadays be given of exercises involving 13 000 troops or 300 battle tanks and, if more than 17 000 are involved, observers must be invited. In the case of an amphibious landing, 3000 troops are enough to require notification and 5000 the invitation of observers.[31] Romania, however, had no success with the proposal (put forward in January 1984) that 30 days' notice should be given of exercises involving more than a dozen surface warships displacing a total of 60 000 tons.[32] Nor did the Soviet Union, in October 1985, with the seemingly easier suggestion for exchanging annual calendars of naval manoeuvres involving 30 ships and 100 aircraft.

From one point of view the Stockholm Conference represented a striking success for the United States. In 1981 the Russians offered to include the European part of the Soviet Union in the area within which confidence-building measures would be applied, provided that this area also included the adjoining seas. The United States and its allies successfully resisted any obligation to notify naval manoeuvres not involving amphibious operations or to allow these to be attended by observers. After Gorbachev had waived the Russian proposal in January 1986, 'the conference solidified agreement on an "Atlantic to the Urals" geographic definition – specifically, on inclusion of all the European territory of the USSR – as the area of application . . . without providing additional compensation in the West as the Soviet Union had requested'.[33]

Nevertheless it would be wishful thinking to regard the so called Stockholm Document – the record of the agreement reached in September 1986 by the states participating in the Conference on Confidence-and-Security-Building Measures and Disarmament in Europe – as the end of the story. Gorbachev's waiver may have been prompted by the reluctance of Soviet admirals to contemplate any constraint on the manoeuvres of the Northern Fleet, but the record of Soviet policy on naval arms control suggests that an eventual return to the issue can be expected. Whether new proposals then prosper will depend on their conformity with the principles suggested by the United Nations Study on the Naval Arms Race: reciprocity of advantage and choosing the right political moment.[34]

These were not the most obvious features of Gorbachev's speech – made, as earlier mentioned, at Murmansk on 1 October 1987. He did indeed propose

limiting the scale of the activity of naval and air forces in the waters of the Baltic, Norwegian and Greenland seas and that confidence-building measures be extended to them . . . notification of major exercises of naval and air forces, and inviting observers from all states participating in the European process to major exercises of these forces.

If we take the Helsinki Conference of 1975 as the yardstick, there are 35 states participating in the European process. Of course, an American aircraft carrier or the Russian battle-cruiser KIROV could accommodate, perhaps not very comfortably, a couple of observers from each, but the psychological stress their presence would cause to the security-minded officers of either ship would be considerable. To appease their apprehensions while sufficiently satisfying the need-to-know of the observers might be no easy task within the constricted space of even the largest warship. Perhaps a cruise liner could be chartered to accompany the task force, thus allowing the observers to watch the manoeuvres, as Captain Pakenham calmly contemplated the battle of Tsushima, from a deck-chair. But would this be enough to build confidence?

Many problems and difficulties of this kind might eventually be overcome by detailed negotiations, but the initial package on offer will have to be made considerably more enticing if even the most pacific of American presidents is to overcome the foreseeable objections of his admirals. What, they will ask, is in it for us?

ARMS CONTROL AND STRATEGY

We must end where we began. It is natural for advocates of arms control to focus their attention on those aspects of naval power which seem most dangerous. They must consider not only which weapons will wreak most destruction, but also which weapons are most likely to be used. The causes of war, moreover, are no less important than its conduct. If there is a risk that the peacetime deployment of navies, or the manoeuvres they practise, or their behaviour at sea or towards the shore, might lead to an otherwise avoidable war, then these, too, are legitimate matters for enquiry, for negotiation and even for agreed restraint.

Not all advocates of arms control, of course, are solely, even mainly, animated by a desire to reduce the incidence or the horror of war. Politicians, no less than admirals, display much ingenuity in devising attractive arguments to advance the interests they support. But anyone concerned with arms control, whether he is for it or against it, a sincere pacifist or a dissembling hawk, must take account of current strategic views. These have not, historically, always been closely related to the real world or to the actual conduct of the next war. But they help to set the scene and to suggest the priorities for the discussion of arms control. Perhaps their contribution is less important than political perceptions of significant popular sentiment, but strategic considerations can never safely be neglected.

For much of the 1950s, 1960s and 1970s, the emphasis of the strategists was on nuclear war. By a peculiar perversion of language, the very word 'strategic' was increasingly confined to a nuclear context. It was commonly assumed, in countries of very different political persuasions, that war between the Super Powers would be not only general, but also total and, therefore, nuclear. These assumptions were reflected in efforts at arms control. Walker's Chronology of proposals from 1963 to 1986 lists well over a hundred concerned with nuclear weapons, compared with a mere 21 on conventional arms control in Europe. And 6 of those in the latter category related to so-called 'tactical' nuclear weapons. Walker describes his chronology as indicative rather than comprehensive, but it is nevertheless remarkable that he has mentioned only one naval proposal *not* concerned with submarine-launched ballistic missiles.[35]

Naturally there were more – the many geographical constraints and confidence-building measures earlier mentioned – but this narrow interpretation of arms control is quite common among official Western analysts – or was in the past. It will be harder to sustain in future, for strategic assumptions are changing. As early as 1980 James McConnell of the US Center for Naval Analyses suggested that Soviet strategic doctrine no longer regarded war between the Super Powers as 'inevitably' total nuclear war. He even predicted eventual Soviet acceptance of purely conventional war as a valid option.[36]

Meanwhile the US Navy have adopted the Maritime Strategy. As argued in the first chapter of this book, it is far from certain that this strategy could be implemented by conventional means alone or that it would encounter a purely conventional response. Nevertheless the strategy has been advocated in the United States as offering an alternative to nuclear war. It is, of course, an alternative that seems rather more attractive on the other side of the Atlantic.

US naval planners look to employ conventional systems even if that means initial setbacks; they look at theaters around the globe, not at one battlefield; they envision a long struggle, perhaps punctuated by episodic ceasefires.[37]

Admiral Sir Nicholas Hunt, formerly NATO C. in C. Channel and Eastern Atlantic, when endorsing the Maritime Strategy, remarked: 'our game is attrition'.[38] So it has been in the Iran–Iraq war – at the moment of writing supposed to have scored a million casualties in seven-and-a-half years. It is scarcely surprising that Admiral Sir James Eberle considered the 'New Maritime Strategy . . . more likely to be welcomed in Europe by Naval officers than it is by political leaders.'[39]

There is no need to develop all the displeasing implications of a long war of naval attrition: the sacrifice of allied forces in Germany, the occupation of much of Western Europe by the Red Army. The main point is obvious. When it comes to the allocation of priorities for arms control among intercontinental nuclear weapons, lesser nuclear weapons, conventional forces on land and conventional forces at sea, it is more than conceivable that the interests and views, not only of Americans and Russians, but of Super Powers and their lesser allies will differ appreciably.

Naturally it is possible to take a more optimistic view of the Maritime Strategy. This may be destined to play the same catalytic role in arms control – even securing Super Power disengagement between the Atlantic and the Urals – as have the East Anglian missiles of the United States in promoting agreement to eliminate weapons of intermediate range.

Such optimists may even be encouraged by Soviet reactions. Although Admiral N. I. Smirnov told *Red Star* on 16 May 1987 that:

The 'new maritime strategy' of the United States is a component of its military doctrine of 'direct confrontation' with the Soviet Union

and feared it would lead 'to the further intensification of the aggressiveness of the US Navy', both General V. Lobov and Admiral Chernavin argued that the Soviet response should take the form of 'far-reaching proposals . . . aimed at limiting naval activity and naval arms'.[40]

It has been the general tendency of this book to argue that navies are more profitably employed in violent peace than they would be in war. It might seem equally obvious that, if war cannot be altogether avoided, then at least limited war must be preferable to total war. Indeed, earlier chapters contain examples to support such a proposition. Unfortunately it may not always and universally be accepted as true, for wars may be limited only in the eyes of the distant beholder. To the Super Powers, for instance, there are attractions in the idea of a geographically limited war, nuclear or conventional, that would exclude their own metropolitan territories from the battlefield. These attractions are less apparent to those who would pay the price of rewards reaped only by their patrons. Europeans should perhaps be forgiven if the thought of a general conventional war confined to their continent and the surrounding seas seems scarcely less terrible than general nuclear war. They may be mistaken in their favourite paradox – the wider and worse the expected war, the more likely it is to be avoided – but the Super Powers have yet to come up with an equally plausible alternative.

Until they do, Britain and France are likely to cling to the strategic submarines that provide them, in the last resort, with an instrument of deterrent escalation. They and other Europeans may want to echo the words of Lord Carrington, then Secretary-General of NATO:

> So many arms control discussions seem concerned only with nuclear weapons . . . they almost seem to suggest that conventional warfare is acceptable.[41]

Perhaps that is what makes the case for violent peace. Naturally it is an untidy state of affairs and its persistence can excite impatience among those born in better times or more fortunate places. The enduring cloud of potential nuclear annihilation may seem intolerable. If terrorism is endemic even in civilised parts, something must be wrong. There is an uneasy sense that prosperity is threatened, evil and anarchy creeping nearer, the world becoming a more disorderly planet. The fears are real, but the surgical remedies sometimes proposed seem worse than the human disease. Nuclear nightmares apart, the experience of the last forty years suggests that the political utility of even conventional war is subject to severe constraints. Unless force can effect an immediate cure, then its prolonged application, even at much increased levels, may only make matters worse: Afghanistan, Central America, the Gulf War, Indochina and the Middle East.

The controlled application of a force that is limited and appropriate does, however, occasionally have a useful result. This cannot often be done at sea, but such opportunities as do arise present navies with a task that is as important and potentially as valuable at the end of the century as it has ever been. Violence cannot be eliminated by ending peace, but there is just a chance that some kind of peace can be preserved by limiting the level of violence.

Notes and References

Introduction
1. Admiral James D. Watkins, *The Maritime Strategy* (Annapolis US Naval Institute, January 1986), p. 5.
2. Quoted from *Red Star* in the *Naval Review* for October 1986.
3. Melvin Small and J. David Singer, *Resort to Arms: International and Civil Wars 1816–1980* (Beverly Hills, Sage Publications Inc., 1982), pp. 293–5.
4. Quoted in Arthur J. Marder, *British Naval Policy 1880–1905* (London, Putnam & Company, 1940), p. 8.
5. Major Greenwood, 'British Loss of Life in the Wars of 1794–1815 and 1914–1918', *Journal of the Royal Statistical Society*, Vol. CV, 1942, p. 15.
6. Baldur Kaulisch, *Alfred von Tirpitz und die Imperialistische Flottenrüstung* (Militärverlag der Deutschen Demokratischen Republik, Berlin, 1982), p. 40; and Marder, *British Naval Policy*, op. cit., p. 7.
7. Marder, *British Naval Policy*, op. cit., p. 123.
8. Ibid., p. 136.
9. Caspar W. Weinberger, *Soviet Military Power* (Washington, Department of Defense, 1987), p. 154.

1 Total War at Sea
1. *Survival*, March/April, 1986, p. 155.
2. Carl Sagan, 'Nuclear War and Climatic Catastrophe' in Fred Holroyd (ed.), *Thinking About Nuclear Weapons* (London, Croom Helm for the Open University, 1985).
3. Joseph S. Nye Jr, 'Nuclear winter and policy choices', *Survival*, March/April 1986.
4. Winston S. Churchill, *The Second World War*, Vol VI (London, Cassell, 1954), p. 554.
5. *The Military Balance 1987–1988* (London, International Institute for Strategic Studies), p. 225.
6. See note 1.
7. *Survival*, July/August 1972, p. 192.
8. *Survival*, March/April 1977, p. 78.
9. Robin F. Laird and Dale R. Herspring, *The Soviet Union and Strategic Arms* (Boulder, Colorado, and London, Westview Press, 1984), p. 24.
10. John van Oudenaren, *Deterrence, War-fighting and Soviet Military Doctrine* (Adelphi Paper no. 210, International Institute for Strategic Studies, London, 1986), p. 7.
11. James Cable, *The Geneva Conference of 1954 on Indochina* (London, Macmillan, 1986), p. 79.
12. Colin Gray quoted in James M. Garrett, 'The Ambiguous Roles of Intermediate Range Theater Nuclear Forces', *Journal of Strategic Studies*, September 1985.
13. Quoted in Paul Stockton, *Strategic Stability between the Super-Powers*

(Adelphi Paper no. 213, International Institute for Strategic Studies, London, 1986).

14. Quoted in *United States Naval Institute Proceedings*, August 1987.
15. Alfred L. Monks, *Soviet Military Doctrine* (New York, Irvington Publications, 1984), p. 303.
16. *Strategic Survey 1985–1986*, (London, International Institute for Strategic Studies, 1986), p. 42.
17. Quoted in Bryan Ranft and Geoffrey Till, *The Sea in Soviet Strategy* (London, Macmillan, 1983), p. 155.
18. Commander John L. Byron, 'Sea Power: The Global Navy', *United States Naval Institute Proceedings*, January 1984.
19. Norman Polmar and Donald M. Kerr, 'Nuclear Torpedoes', *United States Naval Institute Proceedings*, August 1986.
20. Admiral James D. Watkins, *The Maritime Strategy* (Annapolis, US Naval Institute, January 1986).
21. Harold Nicolson, *Lord Carnock* (London, Constable, 1930), pp. 409–16.
22. Quoted in *United States Naval Institute Proceedings*, December 1986.
23. For a fuller account see Stephen S. Roberts, 'The October 1973 Arab–Israeli War' in Bradford Dismukes and James McConnell, *Soviet Naval Diplomacy* (New York, Pergamon Press, 1979).
24. Quoted in Ranft and Till, *The Sea in Soviet Strategy*, op. cit., p. 159.
25. Lord Carver, *Hansard*, House of Lords, Vol. 423, no. 21, Monday 20 July 1981, Col. 59.
26. Alan Bullock, *Hitler: A Study in Tyranny* (London, Odhams Press, 1952), p. 300.
27. Hamlin A. Caldwell, Jr., 'Nuclear War at Sea', *United States Institute Proceedings*, February 1988.

2   Limited War at Sea

1. Quoted in James M. McConnell, 'Gorshkov's Doctrine of Coercive Naval Diplomacy in Both Peace and War' in *Admiral Gorshkov on Navies in War and Peace*, Arlington, Center for Naval Analyses, 1974, p. 103.
2. Quoted in Paul B. Ryan, *First Line of Defense: The US Navy Since 1945* (Stanford, Hoover Institution Press, 1981), p. 55.
3. Robert P. Haffa, Jr, *The Half War: Planning US Rapid Deployment Forces to Meet a Limited Contingency 1960–1983* (Boulder, Westview Press, 1984), p. 237.
4. Melvin Small and J. David Singer, *Resort to Arms: International and Civil Wars 1816–1980* (Beverly Hills, Sage Publications, 2nd ed., 1982).
5. Max Hastings and Simon Jenkins, *The Battle for the Falklands* (London, Michael Jospeh, 1983), p. 316. Another authority suggests 1001: Martin Middlebrook, *Task Force: The Falklands War 1982* (Harmondsworth, Penguin, revised ed., 1987), pp. 383–4.
6. R. E. Dupuy and T. N. Dupuy, *Encyclopaedia of Military History* (London, Jane's Publishing Co., 1980), p. 1227.
7. David Rees, *Korea: The Limited War* (London, Macmillan, 1964), passim.

8. Robert Jackson, *Suez 1956: Operation Musketeer* (London, Ian Allan, 1980), passim.
9. Joseph C. Goulden, *Truth is the First Casualty* (Chicago, Rand, McNally & Co, 1969), passim.
10. Harold James and Denis Sheil-Small, *The Undeclared War* (London, Leo Cooper, 1971), passim.
11. *Strategic Survey 1985–1986* (International Institute for Strategic Studies, London), p. 126.
12. *The Times*, 6 February 1987.
13. *The Times*, 9 May 1987.
14. James Cable, *Diplomacía de Cañoneras* (Buenos Aires, Librería El Ateneo, 1977), p. 7.
15. Middlebrook, *Task Force*, op. cit., p. 67.
16. Ibid., p. 94.
17. Ibid., pp. 145–6.
18. Secretary of State for Defence, *The Falklands Campaign: The Lessons* (London, HMSO, Cmnd 8758, December 1982), p. 15.
19. Admiral James D. Watkins, *The Maritime Strategy* (Annapolis, US Naval Institute, January 1986), p. 5.
20. See Note 1.

3 Proxy War at Sea

1. Speech of 26 July 1978 in Michael Taber (ed.), *Fidel Castro: Speeches* (New York, Pathfinder Press, 1981), p. 53.
2. Townsend Hoopes, *The Devil and John Foster Dulles* (London, André Deutsch, 1974), p. 115.
3. Josef Stalin, 'Party After Seizure of Power', *Pravda*, 28 August 1921.
4. Quoted in Michael Parenti, *The Anti-Communist Impulse* (New York, Random House, 1969), p. 169.
5. Zdanek Cervenka and Colin Legum, 'Cuba: The New Communist Power in Africa' in Legum and Lee, *The Horn of Africa in Continuing Crisis* (New York, Africana, 1979), p. 139.
6. See Robert A. Pastor, 'Cuba and the Soviet Union: Does Cuba Act Alone?' in Barry B. Levine, *The New Cuban Presence in the Caribbean* (Epping, Bowker, 1983), pp. 205–7.
7. Rudyard Kipling, *Kim* (London, Macmillan, 1908), p. 156.
8. Christopher Coker, *NATO, the Warsaw Pact and Africa* (London, Macmillan, 1985), pp. 88–90.
9. Arthur Jay Klinghoffer, *The Angolan War* (Boulder, Colorado, Westview Press, 1980), p. 28.
10. Stephen S. Roberts, 'The October 1973 Arab–Israeli War' in Bradford Dismukes and James McConnell, *Soviet Naval Diplomacy* (New York, Pergamon Press, 1979), passim.
11. Coker, *Nato, the Warsaw Pact and Africa*, op. cit., p. 99.
12. Ibid., p. 109.
13. Max Azicri, 'Cuba and the United States' in Levine, *The New Cuban Presence*, op. cit., p. 187.

4 The Persistence of Gunboat Diplomacy

1. Quoted in James Cable, 'Flicker of An Imperial Flame', *International Relations*, November 1983, p. 2440.
2. Quoted in Anthony Pearson, *Conspiracy of Silence* (London, Quartet Books, 1978), p. 57.
3. Quoted in Tony Thorndike, *Grenada: Politics, Economics and Society* (London, Frances Pinter, 1985), p. 171.
4. James Cable, *Gunboat Diplomacy 1919–1979* (London, Macmillan, 1981), p. 39.
5. For a more extended discussion of coercive diplomacy, see James Cable, *Diplomacy at Sea* (London, Macmillan, 1985).
6. Ken Booth, *Law, Force and Diplomacy at Sea* (London, George Allen & Unwin, 1985), p. 147.
7. For fuller particulars see article cited in Note 1.
8. *Keesing's Contemporary Archives.*
9. *Royal Navy Broadsheet 86*, London, HMSO, 1986, p. 4.
10. *The Times*, 24 January 1986.
11. James Cable, *Gunboat Diplomacy*, op. cit., p. 19.
12. Anthony Pearson, *Conspiracy of Silence*, op. cit., passim.
13. James M. Eames, Jr, *Assault on the* LIBERTY (New York, Random House, 1979), Foreword.
14. Joseph C. Goulden, *Truth is the First Casualty* (Chicago, Rand, McNally, 1969), p. 143.
15. Richard K. Smith, 'The Violation of the LIBERTY', *United States Naval Institute Proceedings*, June 1978.
16. Anthony Pearson, *Conspiracy of Silence*, op. cit., passim.
17. See Note 15.
18. Trevor Armbrister, *A Matter of Accountability: The True Story of the* PUEBLO *Affair* (London, Barrie & Jenkins, 1970), p. 139.
19. Goulden, *Truth is the First Casualty*, op. cit., p. 215.
20. James Cable, *Gunboat Diplomacy*, op. cit., pp. 50–57 and 83–4.
21. J.A.S. Grenville, *Lord Salisbury and Foreign Policy* (London, Athlone Press, 1970), p. 295.
22. Lord Franks, *Falkland Islands Review* (London, HMSO, 1983), pp. 11–12. Lord Shackleton, for whose father the ship was named, had just aroused Argentine anger by visiting the Falkland Islands to conduct an enquiry.
23. Pearson, *Conspiracy of Silence*, op. cit., pp. 56–7.
24. Cable, *Gunboat Diplomacy*, op. cit., p. 246.
25. A book written with the help of the US Department of State argues that, once aboard GUAM, Scoon merely gave written confirmation of a plea for help made through an intermediary just before the landing began. Gregory Sandford and Richard Vigilante, *Grenada: The Untold Story* (Lanham, Madison Books, 1984), pp. 8–9.
26. Thorndike, *Grenada*, op. cit., p. 65.
27. Scott Davidson, *Grenada* (Aldershot, Gower, 1987), p. 32; *The Times* 7 November 1983.
28. Thorndike, *Grenada*, op. cit., pp. 128–9.
29. Ibid, p. 164.

30. Frank Uhlig, Jr, 'Amphibious Aspects of the Grenada Episode' in Peter M. Dunn and Bruce W. Watson (eds), *American Intervention in Grenada* (Boulder, Westview Press, 1985), pp. 89–97.
31. Lawrence S. Germain, 'A Chronology of Events Concerning Grenada' in Dunn, and Watson, *American Intervention*, op. cit., pp. 163–75.
32. Dorothea Cypher, 'Urgent Fury: The US Army in Grenada' in Dunn and Watson, *American Intervention*, op. cit., p. 107.
33. G. F. Illingworth, 'Grenada in Retrospect' in Dunn and Watson, *American Intervention*, op. cit., p. 136.
34. Thorndike, *Grenada*, op. cit., pp. 172–4.
35. See Note 31.
36. Secretary of State for Defence, *The Falklands Campaign: The Lessons* (London, HMSO, Cmnd 8758, 1982); and Martin Middlebrook *Task Force: The Falklands War 1982* (Harmondsworth, Penguin, revised ed. 1987, passim).
37. See Note 30.
38. Davidson, *Grenada*, op. cit., pp. 138–49.
39. Sandford and Vigilante *Grenada: the Untold Story*, op. cit., say the US Ambassador in *Barbados* recommended evacuation on 19 October and sent members of his staff to Grenada on the 22nd to try to arrange this with the Government of Grenada. Agreement was not reached and the US authorities feared US citizens might eventually be treated as hostages. The authors do not mention any contact with US citizens in Grenada or suggest that these were in imminent danger before the invasion.
40. James Cable, *The Royal Navy and the Siege of Bilbao* (Cambridge University Press, 1979), passim.
41. Dorothea Cypher in Dunn and Watson, *American Intervention*, op. cit., p. 106.
42. James Adams, *Secret Armies* (London, Hutchinson, 1987), pp. 221–55.

5 Gunboat Diplomacy in the 1980s and Beyond

1. Yuri Barsegov and Artemi Sagiryan, 'US Naval Provocations and International Law', *International Affairs* (Moscow), March 1987.
2. Speech by President Reagan at the recommissioning of the battleship NEW JERSEY in December 1982.
3. Quoted in *United States Naval Institute Proceedings*, August 1979.
4. James Cable, *Gunboat Diplomacy* (London, Chatto & Windus, 1971), p. 49.
5. Quoted in *United States Naval Institute Proceedings*, February 1981.
6. Captain James F. Kelly, USN, 'Naval Deployment in the Indian Ocean', *United States Naval Institute Proccedings*, May 1983.
7. Secretary of State for Defence, *Statement on the Defence Estimates 1981* (London, HMSO, Cmnd 8212–I), p. 32.
8. *Keesing's Contemporary Archives*.
9. See Note 7.
10. Sir Adrian Swire, 'Merchant Shipping and the Gulf War', *Naval Forces*, No. III, 1987.
11. Nick Childs, 'The Naval Stakes in the Gulf', *Navy International*, October 1987.

12. See Note 6.
13. *Guardian* 24 July 1987, quoting US Congressional Research Service.
14. *The Times*, 3 September 1987.
15. *The Times*, 8 June 1984.
16. Third Special Report from the Defence Committee of the House of Commons, *The Protection of British Merchant Shipping in the Persian Gulf*, 13 May 1987, London, HMSO.
17. *The Times*, 10 September 1987.
18. *The Times*, 17 December 1987.
19. *The Times*, 22 October 1987.
20. *The Times*, 21 November 1987.
21. *Independent*, 17 November 1987.
22. *The Times*, 11 December 1987.
23. *The Times*, 12 December 1987.
24. Jeffrey Schloesser (Bureau of Near East and South Asian Affairs), 'US Policy in the Persian Gulf', *Department of State Bulletin*, Vol. 87, No. 2127, Washington, October 1987.
25. Admiral James D. Watkins, *The Maritime Strategy* (US Naval Institute, Annapolis, 1986).
26. *Independent*, 18 December 1987.
27. *The Times*, 26 December 1987; 28 December 1987; 31 December 1987; 2 January 1988.
28. James Cable, *The Royal Navy and the Siege of Bilbao* (Cambridge University Press, 1979), passim.
29. Hugh Thomas, *The Spanish Civil War* (London, Eyre & Spottiswood, 1961), p. 293.
30. Although a helicopter from HMS EXETER did help to rescue wounded sailors from the HAVGLIMT after this Singapore-registered Norwegian tanker had been attacked by Iranian gunboats: *The Times*, 23 March 1988.

6 Showing the Flag

1. Arthur Bryant, *Samuel Pepys: The Saviour of the Navy* (London, Collins, 1938), p. 106.
2. Arthur Bryant, *Samuel Pepys: The Years of Peril* (London, Collins, 1948), p. 119.
3. D. P. O'Connell, *The International Law of the Sea* (Oxford, Clarendon Press, 1982), p. 9.
4. Thomas Campbell, 'Ye Mariners of England', *The Oxford Book of English Verse* (Oxford, Clarendon Press, 1931), p. 673.
5. According to *The International Herald Tribune* of 20 March 1986, US officials admitted the two ships were within 6 miles of the coast on 13 March. For the later Crimean incident, see *The Times* of 13 and 15 February 1988, *The Sunday Times* of 14 February and *The International Herald Tribune* of 15 February 1988.
6. *The Times*, 20 February 1985. See also *Report by the Submarine Defence Commission – Countering the submarine threat: Submarine violations and Swedish Security Policy*, tr. Keith Bradfield, Stockholm, Ministry of Defence, 1983.

7. *Jane's Defence Weekly*, 31 October 1987.
8. Hervé Coutau-Bégarie, *Géostratégie du Pacifique* (Economica, Paris, 1987), pp. 126, 197.
9. Quoted in *United States Naval Institute Proceedings*, December 1986.
10. Christopher C. Wright, 'US Naval Operations in 1986', *US Naval Institute Proceedings*, May 1987.
11. Report of the Secretary-General to the General Assembly A/40/535, 17 September 1985, United Nations, New York, p. 72.
12. See Note 9.
13. *US Naval Institute Proceedings*, May 1976.
14. *The Times*, 27 October 1982.
15. Paul Kennedy, *Strategy and Diplomacy 1870–1945* (London, Fontana, 1984), p. 130.
16. Arthur J. Marder, *Old Friends, New Enemies: The Royal Navy and the Imperial Japanese Navy* (Oxford University Press, 1981), p. 7.
17. Anthony Verrier, *Through the Looking Glass* (London, Jonathan Cape, 1983), pp. 135–6.
18. *US Naval Institute Proceedings*, February 1987.
19. Ken Booth, *Navies and Foreign Policy* (London, Croom Helm, 1977), p. 64.

7 Estate Management at Sea

1. Quoted in D. P. O'Connell, *The International Law of the Sea*, Vol. I (Oxford, Clarendon Press, 1982), p. 113.
2. Rear-Admiral J. R. Hill, *Maritime Strategy for Medium Powers* (London, Croom Helm, 1986), p. 99.
3. Geoffrey Till, *Maritime Strategy and the Nuclear Age* (London, Macmillan, 2nd ed., 1984), p. 203.
4. *The Military Balance 1986–1987* (International Institute for Strategic Studies, London, 1986).
5. Extract from Article 26 *of Statute on the Protection of the State Boundary of the Union of Soviet Socialist Republics* in William E. Butler, *The Law of Soviet Territorial Waters* (New York, Praeger, 1967).
6. See Note 4.
7. Alvin Moscow, *Collision Course* (London, Longman, 1959), p. 173.
8. Till *Maritime Strategy*, op. cit., p. 227.
9. *The Times*, 14 September 1985.
10. O'Connell, *International Law*, op. cit., p. 36.
11. Nien-Tsu Alfred Hu, 'The Sino-Argentine "Squid War" of 1986' in *Marine Policy*, Vol. II, No. 2, April 1987; *The Times* 21 May 1986.
12. *The Times* 13 August 1985; 12 and 20 September 1985; and David L. VanderZwaag, *The Fish Feud*, Aldershot, Gower, 1984, p. 67. Ted L. McDorman, 'In the Wake of the POLAR SEA', *Marine Policy*, October 1986. Captain Thomas C. Pullen, 'What Price Canadian Sovereignty?', *US Naval Institute Proceedings*, September 1987.
13. O'Connell, *International Law*, op. cit., pp. 317–18.
14. Speech of 2 September 1901.
15. *The Times*, 28 April 1983.

16. A 1983 estimate by *Time* quoted in Ken Booth, *Law, Force and Diplomacy at Sea* (London, George Allen & Unwin, 1985), p. 131.
17. James Cable, *Gunboat Diplomacy 1919–1979* (London, Macmillan, 1981), passim.
18. O'Connell, *International Law*, op. cit., p. 319.
19. Carlos E. Hernandez Gonzales, 'The CALDAS Incident: The View from Caracas', *United States Naval Institute Proceedings*, March 1988.
20. *The Times*, 18 November 1986 and 27/28 October 1987.
21. *Independent*, 18 December 1987.
22. *The Times*, 6 October 1987.
23. *The Times*, 29 November 1986.
24. *The Times*, 3 May 1986. It is not only the Super Powers that find the problems of submarine navigation daunting. A West German submarine crashed into a North Sea oil-rig in March 1988: *The Times* 7 and 8 March 1988.
25. *The Times*, 19 and 20 October 1987.
26. Secretary of State for Defence, *Statement on the Defence Estimates 1982*, Part 2, (London, HMSO, Cmnd 8529–II, 1982), p. 61.
27. *The Times*, 8 March 1984.
28. *The Times*, 16 October 1986.
29. John Farnell and James Elles, *In Search of a Common Fisheries Policy* (Aldershot, Gower, 1984), p. 160.
30. VanderZwaag, *The Fish Feud*, op. cit., p. xi.
31. *The Times* 19 April 1988.
32. James Cable, *Gunboat Diplomacy*, op. cit., p. 20.
33. Booth, *Law, Force and Diplomacy*, op. cit., pp. 21–23.
34. Ibid., p. 38.

8 Piracy and Terrorism at Sea

1. Quoted in D. P. O'Connell, *The International Law of the Sea*, Vol. II (Oxford, Clarendon Press, 1984), p. 967.
2. Ibid., p. 969.
3. Ibid., p. 967.
4. For this ironical footnote to recent history I am indebted to an unpublished thesis by Admiral Hill on 'The Rule of Law at Sea'.
5. See Barry H. Dubner, *The Law of International Sea Piracy* (The Hague, Martinus Nijhoff, 1980), pp. 147–9, and P. W. Birnie, 'Piracy: past, present and future', *Marine Policy*, July 1987.
6. Edward F. Mickolus, *Transnational Terrorism: A Chronology of Events 1968–1979* (London, Aldwych Press, 1980), p. 164.
7. Ibid., p. 546.
8. Ibid., p. 878.
9. See Note 5 and Rainer Osterwalder, 'Rescue in the South China Sea', *Swiss Review of World Affairs*, January 1988.
10. *The Times* 11 and 14 February 1986; Scott C. Turner, 'Maritime Terrorism 1985', *United States Naval Institute Proceedings* May 1986.
11. *Keesing's Contemporary Archives* and *Facts on File*.
12. Captain Donald Macintyre, *The Privateers*, London, Paul Elek, 1975, p. 184.

13. Ibid., p. 187.
14. *Independent*, 15 October 1987.
15. Hugh Thomas, *The Spanish Civil War* (London, Eyre & Spottiswoode, 1961), p. 477.
16. US Department of State, 'Patterns of Global Terrorism 1984' *Terrorism*, Vol. 9, No. 4, 1987.
17. Jan S. Breemer, 'Offshore Energy Terrorism', *Terrorism*, Vol. 6, No. 3, 1983.
18. *Daily Telegraph*, 16 March 1983.
19. *The Times*, 19 September 1987.
20. *The Times*, 4 February 1988.
21. *The Times*, 20 October, 1986. *Guardian*, 1 November 1986.

9 Who Needs Ocean-going Navies?

1. Admiral of the Fleet Sergei Gorshkov, *The Sea Power of the State* (London, Pergamon, 1979), p. 180.
2. Admiral James D. Watkins, *The Maritime Strategy* (Annapolis, UN Naval Institute, 1986).
3. The Labour Party, *Defence Conversion and Costs*, London, September 1986, p. 36.
4. *Royal Navy Broadsheet 1987*, Eastcote CS(Rep S)LP, p. 4.
5. *Jane's Defence Weekly*, 24 October 1987.
6. Hervé Coutau-Bégarie, *Géostratégie du Pacifique* (Paris, Economica, 1987), p. 207.
7. *Naval Forces*, No. IV, 1986, Vol. VII.
8. Robert Browning, 'Andrea del Sarto', *The Poems of Robert Browning* (Oxford University Press, 1936), p. 132.
9. James Cable, *Gunboat Diplomacy 1919–1979* (London, Macmillan, 1981), p. 203.
10. Caspar W. Weinberger, Secretary of Defense, *Soviet Military Power 1987* (Washington, US Government Printing Office), p. 85.
11. Ibid., p. 87.
12. Ibid., p.149.
13. *The Times*, 28 February 1986.
14. A. A. Gromyko and B. N. Ponomarev, *Soviet Foreign Policy*, Vol. II, 1945–1980, tr. David Svirsky (Moscow, Progress Publishers, 4th ed., 1981), p. 520.
15. Lieutenant de Vaisseau Robert L. Cogné, 'France's Global Reach', *US Naval Institute Proceedings*, March 1987.
16. Vice-Admiral V. E. C. Barboza, 'The Development of the Indian Ocean as a Naval Theatre', *Naval Forces*, No. IV/1986, Vol. VII.
17. Rear-Admiral J. R. Hill, *Maritime Strategy for Medium Powers* (London, Croom Helm, 1986), p. 97.
18. Major-General Edward Furdson, 'Exercise Saif Sareea and Out of Area Operations', *Navy International*, March 1987.
19. *Royal Navy Broadsheet 1986*, Southampton, HMSO, 1986, pp. 9–10.
20. Secretary of State of Defence, *The United Kingdom Defence Programme: The Way Forward* (London, HMSO, Cmnd 8288, 1981), p. 8;

138   *Notes and References*

10   Arms Control at Sea
 1. Viscount Grey of Fallodon, *Twenty-Five Years, 1892–1916*, Vol. I. (London, Hodder & Stoughton, 1925), pp. 91–2.
 2. Ken Booth, *Law, Force and Diplomacy at Sea* (London, George Allen & Unwin, 1985), p. 216.
 3. Report of the Secretary-General: *Study on the naval arms race* (General Assembly of the United Nations A/40/535 of 1985).
 4. Winston S. Churchill, *The World Crisis 1911–1918* (London, Landsborough Publications, 1960), p. 79.
 5. Report by Count Metternich of 16 July 1908, quoted in David Lloyd George, *War Memoirs*, Vol. I, (London, Odhams Press, 1938), p. 11.
 6. *Strategic Survey 1986–1987* (London, IISS, 1987), p. 59.
 7. Francis J. West, Jr, Jacquelyn K. Davis, James E. Dougherty, Robert J. Hanks and Charles M. Perry, *Naval Forces and Western Security* (Washington, Pergamon-Brasseys, 1986), p. 43. See also E. F. Gueritz, Norman Friedman, Clarence A. Robinson, Will R. Van Cleeve, *NATO's Maritime Strategy: Issues and Developments* (Washington, Pergamon-Brasseys, 1987), pp. 45–62. The Russians *did* revert to the topic. *International Herald Tribune*, 15 February 1988.
 8. Gueritz et al., *Nato's Maritime Strategy*, op. cit., p. 46.
 9. *Strategic Survey 1985–1986*, op. cit., p. 237.
10. Report of the Secretary-General, op. cit., p. 11.
11. Anthony R. Deluca, *Great Power Rivalry at the Turkish Straits: The Montreux Conference and Convention of 1936* (New York, Columbia University Press), 1981, p. 7.
12. Barry Buzan, 'The Status and Future of the Montreux Convention', *Survival*, November–December 1976.
13. Secretary of State for Defence, *Statement on the Defence Estimates 1979*, (London, HMSO, Cmnd 7474), p. 30.
14. Commander I. A. Scrymgeour-Wedderburn, RN Retd, letter to *The Times*, 24 September 1984.
15. *The Times*, 27 March 1986 and 17 March 1988.
16. *The Times*, 29 December 1987 and 15 March 1988.
17. *The Times*, 28 November 1986.
18. Lev Vtorygin, 'Maritime Law and Naval Arms Limitation: A Soviet Perspective', in R. B. Byers (ed.), *The Denuclearisation of the Oceans* (London, Croom Helm, 1986).
19. Report of the Secretary-General, op. cit., p. 30.
20. Admiral James D. Watkins, *The Maritime Strategy* (Annapolis, US Naval Institute, 1986).
21. George Orwell, *Animal Farm* (London, Secker & Warburg, 1945), p. 87.
22. James Cable, *The Royal Navy and the Siege of Bilbao* (Cambridge University Press, 1979), p. 147.
23. Richard Haass, 'Confidence Building Measures and Naval Arms Control', in *Confidence-Building Measures* (Adelphi Paper no. 149, London International Institute for Strategic Studies, 1979).
24. The Soviet–British Incidents at Sea Agreement text in *Naval Forces*, No. 1/1987, Vol. VIII, pp. 14–15.
25. Grey of Fallodon *Twenty-Five Years*, op. cit., pp. 13–15.

26. James Cable, *The Royal Navy and the Siege of Bilbao*, op. cit., pp. 146–7. The incident turned on a 'nice point' in international law. If the British ship GORDONIA had escaped to the high seas after being challenged by ALMIRANTE CERVERA *inside* Spanish territorial waters, did RESOLUTION have the right to protect her from renewed challenge *outside*?

27. Stephen S. Roberts, 'Superpower Naval Confrontation', in Bradford Dismukes and James McConnell, *Soviet Naval Diplomacy* (New York, Pergamon Press, 1979), p. 204.

28. Ibid., p. 176.

29. Gueritz et al., *NATO's Maritime Strategy*, op. cit., pp. 23–44. For a more optimistic view of this Agreement and an interesting commentary on the whole subject see Hervé Coutau-Bégarie, 'Une Limitation des Armements Navals, Est-Elle Possible?', *Défense Nationale*, February 1988.

30. Richard Haass quoted in J. Borawski, 'Risk Reduction at Sea: Naval Confidence-Building Measures', *Naval Forces*, No. 1/1987, Vol. VIII.

31. Document of the Stockholm Conference on Confidence-and-Security-Building Measures and Disarmament in Europe, 19 September 1986, in *Survival*, January/February 1987.

32. John Walker, 'Arms Control Proposals Chronology 1963–1968', *Royal United Services Institute & Brassey's Defence Yearbook 1987* (Brassey's Defence Publications, London, 1987), p. 422.

33. Richard E. Darilek, 'The Future of Conventional Arms Control in Europe', *SIPRI Yearbook 1987*, Oxford University Press, 1987, p. 343.

34. See Note 19.

35. *RUSI and Brassey's Yearbook*, op. cit., pp. 403–30.

36. James McConnell, 'The Interacting Evolution of Soviet and American Military Doctrines', Memorandum of 17 September 1980, Center for Naval Analyses, Alexandria, USA.

37. Francis J. West, Jr 'US Naval Forces and NATO Planning', in *Naval Forces and Western Security*, op. cit., p. 7.

38. Quoted in Desmond Wettern, 'NATO's Maritime Strategy', *Navy International*, September 1987.

39. Admiral Sir James Eberle, Editorial, *Naval Forces*, No. LV/1986, Vol. VII.

40. Captain William Manthorpe, USN, 'The Soviet View', *United States Naval Institute Proceedings*, November 1987.

41. Quoted in *Arms Control and Disarmament*, the quarterly review of the Arms Control and Disarmament Research Unit, London, Foreign and Commonwealth Office, July 1987, p. 12.

Select Bibliography

1 Periodicals
Défense Nationale (monthly)
Independent, The (daily)
Jane's Defence Weekly
Jane's Fighting Ships (annual)
Keesing's Contemporary Archives (annual)
Marine Policy (quarterly)
Military Balance (annual)
Naval Forces (bi-monthly)
Naval Review (quarterly)
Navy International (monthly)
Royal Navy Broadsheet (annual)
Royal United Services Institute and Brassey's Defence Yearbook
SIPRI Yearbook – World Armament and Disarmament
Soviet Military Power (annual)
Statement on the Defence Estimates (annual)
Strategic Survey (annual)
Survival (bi-monthly)
The Times (daily)
United States Naval Institute Proceedings (monthly)

2 Books
Barber, James A., Jr (ed.), *The Maritime Strategy* (Annapolis, US Naval Institute, 1986).
Booth, Ken, *Law, Force and Diplomacy at Sea* (London, George Allen & Unwin, 1985).
Booth, Ken, *Navies and Foreign Policy* (London, Croom Helm, 1977).
Cable, James, *Diplomacy at Sea* (London, Macmillan, 1985).
Cable, James, *Gunboat Diplomacy 1919–1979* (London, Macmillan, 1981).
Cable, James, *The Royal Navy and the Siege of Bilbao* (Cambridge University Press, 1979).
Coutau-Bégarie, Hervé, *Géostratégie du Pacifique* (Paris, Economica, 1987).
Davidson, Scott, *Grenada* (Aldershot, Gower, 1987).
Dismukes, Bradford and McConnell, James (eds), *Soviet Naval Diplomacy* (New York, Pergamon Press, 1979).
Dunn, Peter M. and Watson, Bruce W. (eds), *American Intervention in Grenada* (Boulder, Colorado, Westview Press, Inc., 1985).
Gorshkov, Admiral of the Fleet, Sergei, *The Sea Power of the State* (London, Pergamon Press, 1979).
Goulden, Joseph C., *Truth is the First Casualty* (Chicago, Rand McNally & Co., 1969).
Gromyko, A. A. and Ponomarev, B. N. (eds), *Soviet Foreign Policy*, Vol. II, *1945–1980* (tr. David Svirsky) (Moscow, Progress Publishers, 4th ed., 1981).

Hill, Rear-Admiral, J. R., *Maritime Strategy for Medium Powers* (London, Croom Helm, 1986).

Marder, Arthur J., *British Naval Policy 1880–1905* (London, Putnam, 1940).

Marder, Arthur J., *Old Friends, New Enemies: The Royal Navy and the Imperial Japanese Navy* (Oxford University Press, 1981).

Middlebrook, Martin, *Task Force: The Falklands War 1982* (Harmondsworth, Penguin Books, rev. ed., 1987).

O'Connell, D. R., *The International Law of the Sea* (Oxford, Clarendon Press, 1982).

Pearson, Anthony, *Conspiracy of Silence: The Attack on the* USS LIBERTY (London, Quartet Books, 1978).

Ranft, Bryan and Till, Geoffrey, *The Sea in Soviet Strategy* (London, Macmillan, 1983).

Sandford, Gregory and Vigilante, Richard, *Grenada: The Untold Story* (Lanham, Madison Books, 1984).

Secretary-General of the United Nations, *Study on the Naval Arms Race* (New York, United Nations, 1985).

Thomas, Hugh, *The Spanish Civil War* (London, Eyre & Spottiswoode, 1961).

Thorndike, Tony, *Grenada: Politics, Economics and Society* (London, Frances Pinter, 1985).

Till, Geoffrey, *Maritime Strategy and the Nuclear Age* (London, Macmillan, 2nd ed., 1984).

Index

Ships mentioned in the text are listed under *Named ships*.

Aden 22, 44
Afghanistan 34, 36, 53, 58, 67, 120, 128
Africa 32, 34–6, 40, 94, 104
Aircraft
    airborne operations 25, 51
    bombers 5, 8, 22–3, 52
    fighters 14, 27, 94
    Harriers 27
    helicopters 19, 21, 51–2, 60, 64
    miscellaneous 29, 37
    & pirates 95
    & terrorism 98–9
    & warships 26, 34, 73, 86
Aircraft carriers
    battle groups 10, 14, 16, 51, 59, 63, 65, 68, 72–3, 101
    operations 19–22, 34–5, 51, 60, 117–18
    pseudonyms 118
    & strategy 5, 8, 10
    & terrorism 94
    & war 18, 22, 25, 103
Albania 86
Algeria 32, 89
Angola 32, 35–7, 78
Antarctic 29, 104, 121
Arabian Sea 22, 60, 63, 66, 109–10
Arab–Israeli War (1948) 17
Arab–Israeli War (1967) 15, 17–18, 21–2, 43, 45–8
Arab–Israeli War (1973) 8, 11, 13, 17, 21–2, 29, 34, 40
Arctic ocean 84–5, 121
Argentina (*see also* Falklands)
    Admiral Massera 48
    & Britain 24–7, 29, 37, 48, 55
    & Chile 30, 37
    & Cuba 37
    'dirty war' 17
    General Galtieri 11
    Junta 25, 37

navy 24–8, 31, 37, 48, 82, 84, 91, 104
Operation Rosario 24–5, 37, 57
Arms control
    Anglo-German Naval Agreement of 1935 114
    armaments 112–17
    arms race 112, 116, 120
    chronology 126
    confidence-building measures 123–5
    deployment 113, 117–21, 125
    geographical approach 117, 121, 123
    Hague conferences 116
    Montreux Convention of 1936 117–18
    naval conduct in peace 113, 117, 122–5
    neglect of naval aspects 114–17
    nuclear 4, 115–17, 120, 123
    prevention of incidents 122–3
    priorities 126–7
    Salt II 115–16
    at sea x
    size of navies 113
    verification 115–16
    Washington Treaty of 1922 114
    zone of peace 119–21
Atlantic ocean 9, 14, 29, 35, 90
Australia 18, 21, 37, 60, 66, 82, 89, 104, 110

Baltic sea 12, 76, 103, 124–5
Battle
    battlefield 17
    Coronel 3
    Dogger Bank 3
    Falklands (1914) 3
    of first salvo 10, 29
    Jutland 3
    Matapan 3

Battle – *continued*
  as objective 13
  Pearl Harbor 11, 15
  Tsushima 3, 30, 125
Belgium 64, 109
Black sea 73, 76, 78, 118
Blockade 18, 20–2, 29, 87
Bombardment 20–1, 25–7, 69
Booth, Ken, (1943–) British
  writer 91, 112, 132 n.6
Brazil 37, 58, 83, 92, 94, 104
Brezhnev, L.I. (1906–82), Soviet
  President 4, 58, 120
Britain (British)
  Admiralty xi, 71, 76, 79, 122
  & Argentina 11, 24–7, 29, 37, 48,
    55
  British seas 71, 87–9
  Coast Guard 83
  Commonwealth 20–1, 51
  flag 71
  free fall of shipbuilding 108
  governments 1, 13, 19, 25, 42–3,
    48, 87, 113
  international role 19, 32, 54, 58–
    9, 92, 106, 108–10
  Labour Party 62, 102
  merchant ships 22, 27, 35, 44, 54,
    62, 108
  Ministry of Defence 13, 27–8, 60,
    62, 89, 97, 111, 118
  oil 41–3, 89, 99–100
  & Persian Gulf 58–70
  Royal Air Force 83
  Royal Marines 24, 44, 87, 89, 99
  strategy 4, 106, 110, 128
  & US 4, 25–6, 37, 53, 64, 110,
    119, 127
British Navy (*see also* Named
    ships)
  admirals xi, 79, 110, 122, 127
  arms control 113–14, 122
  coastal duties 83–4, 89, 99–100
  & deterrence 4–8, 111
  economies 28
  Far East 21–2, 102, 109–10
  First Flotilla 26
  & gunboat diplomacy 39, 41–4,
    54–5, 58, 60, 62–6, 68–70

history xi, 3, 11, 16, 18–22, 24–
    8, 69–70, 92, 100, 113–14, 122
  Naval Review 77
  ocean going 102–3, 105–6, 108–
    10
  reduction of 25, 100, 106
  reviews xi, 77
  Scapa Flow 114
  soulless bureaucrat in 26
  & Spain 54, 69–70, 122
  submarines 4, 8, 110, 128
  in war 24–8, 31, 110
Brown, Harold (1927–): US
  Secretary of Defense 59
Bulgaria 84

Canada 82, 84–5, 90, 110
Caribbean sea 49, 51–2, 57, 92, 94,
    96, 99
Carter, James Earl (1924–): US
  President 45, 49–50, 60, 120
Castro, Fidel (1927–): Cuban
  President 32–3, 37, 39, 50
Chatfield, Admiral of the Fleet Lord
    (1873–1967) 69, 122
Chernavin, Admiral of the Fleet
    V.N. (1928–): C.inC. Soviet
    Navy 6, 12, 127
Chile 30, 37, 53, 104
China
  & gunboat diplomacy 40, 43, 53–
    5, 57, 66, 77, 105
  & Korea 18–19
  Mao Tse Tung 33
  navy xii, 5, 28, 31, 55, 104
  South China sea 95, 98
  & Soviet Union 33, 74, 97
  & Vietnam 19–20, 36, 78
Churchill, Winston (1874–1965) 2,
    13, 39, 42, 76, 113, 129 n.4
Coastal states
  coast guards 28, 82–5
  defence of 28, 44–5, 82, 86, 102
  & foreign warships 85–6, 88
  & navies 28, 86, 89, 102
  territorial waters 44, 82–91
Conflict
  containment of 6, 40

Conflict – *continued*
  future xii, 3, 9, 28, 30, 88, 91
  incidence of ix, 30, 58
  low intensity xii, 57
  naval 9, 76
  overseas x, 21
  & war 16–17, 30
Coutau-Bégarie, Hervé (1957–):
  French writer 74, 135 n.8,
  139 n.29
Cuba
  crisis of 1962 12, 29, 35, 53, 123
  & Grenada 49–51, 53
  navy 74
  overseas intervention 32–7
  & Soviet Union 32–5, 74, 76, 79
  & US 33, 49–51, 53, 99
Cyprus x, 44, 55, 61, 94

Denmark 88–9
Deterrence 4–7, 9–10, 14–15, 26,
  111
Disarmament *see* Arms control
Dominican Republic 44, 55
Egypt 13, 15, 19, 21–2, 34–5, 38,
  43, 80, 90, 94–5, 119
Eisenhower, D.D. (1890–1969): US
  President 4, 58, 79
Estate management
  continental shelf 82, 84
  exclusive economic zones 30, 82,
  102
  good order 82, 86–9
  Lord of the Waste 82, 89
  resource enjoyment 82, 84, 89–
  91
  sovereignty 82, 84–6
  territorial waters 82–91
  & warships x, 83–8
Ethiopia 32, 34–5, 67
Europe
  arms control in 7, 113–8, 123–5
  Economic Community 87, 90
  expansion 30, 102
  & war x, 7, 9, 110, 127–8

Falklands War of 1982
  Admiral Anaya 25, 27, 30
  aftermath 84, 91

  & Booth 112
  casualties 16–17, 24, 52
  & gunboat diplomacy 24, 30, 37,
  57
  Menéndez, General 27
  Operation Corporate 27, 103
  Port Stanley 24–7
  San Carlos Water 26
  surprise in 11
  Task Unit 318.1 26, 37
  undeserving of contemplation
  112
  unique xi, 18, 27, 103
  United Nations 25, 37, 55
Finland 87, 125
First World War
  aftermath 114, 116
  antecedents xi, 11–12, 113–14
  battles 3
  casualties xi
  Schlieffen Plan 14
Fisher, Admiral of the Fleet, Lord
  (1841–1920) xi, 112
Fishing
  autonomous action 86–7, 89
  Dogger Bank 47
  Iceland 58, 86, 89
  protection 58, 86–7, 89–90, 101
Formosa (Taiwan) 33, 97
France (*see also* French Navy)
  Clemenceau 19
  disclosure 1
  fishing 86–7, 90, 101
  French dog 44
  de Gaulle 53
  & Indochina 19–20, 36
  international role 13, 19, 34, 54,
  108–10
  Médecins du Monde 93
  merchant ships 64, 66
  President Mitterrand 79
  revolution of 1789 xi, 81
  strategy 4–5, 109
  war 4, 13, 28, 32
French Navy (*see also* Named ships)
  admirals 112, 122
  aircraft carriers 5, 63
  Bizerta 55
  & deterrence 4–5

French Navy – *continued*
& disarmament 114
Djibouti 44, 108
Free French 79
& gunboat diplomacy 44, 54–5
in Gulf 58, 62–4, 66, 103
history 19–20, 31, 79, 89, 93–4, 122
ocean going 103, 108–10
presence 108–9
submarines 4

German Navy (*see also* Named ships)
distant deployment 103–4
High Seas Fleet 113–14
history 3, 113–14, 136 n.24
showing the flag 77
size 82, 108
& Spain 54
war 3, 28, 31
Germany
Cap Anamur committee 93
Dresden 2
East 82
history 54, 69, 77, 114, 116
merchant ships 61
Nürnberg trials 17
war x, 2, 5, 9, 11–12, 14, 16, 110, 114, 116, 127
West 82
Gibraltar 38, 74, 88
Gorbachev, Mikhail (1931–):
Soviet leader ix, 1, 3–4, 15, 115, 119–21, 124
Gorshkov, Admiral of the Fleet S.G. (1910–88): 80, 102, 112
Great War *see* First World War
Greece x, 38, 54, 58, 82, 89, 91, 94, 105, 119
Greenpeace 88–90
Grenada
Bishop, Maurice 50
casualties 51–2
government 49
island 49
Operation Amber 50, 74
Operation Grenada 39, 89
Operation Urgent Fury 51–3, 57, 89, 133 n.39

Scoon, Sir Paul 49, 51–2, 132 n.25
Guatemala 35
Guinea 35, 87
Guinea-Bissau 32
Gulf States (*see also* Iran, Iraq) 23, 30, 35, 59, 61–2, 65, 67, 90
Gulf War (1980–)
Armilla Patrol 60, 62–4
casualties 23–4, 61, 66, 127
gunboat diplomacy in 57–70
land fighting 14, 58
naval aspects 23–4, 61–70, 97
& oil 23–4, 61–2, 66–7, 90
outside navies xi, 23, 29–30, 35, 58–70, 103–5, 109–10, 128
Straits of Hormuz 23, 60, 64
& Super Powers 34–5
Swire, Sir Adrian 61–2
Gunboat diplomacy
& antiquarians 40
catalytic 59–60
definition 24, 39, 71
definitive 24
elegance 44
evacuation 43–5, 53, 59
evolution of 40–1, 43–5, 52–6, 66, 70
expressive 71
future of 30, 70, 91, 111, 128
instances 24, 30, 39–70, 84–7, 89–91, 105
limited naval force 24, 52, 59–60
oil 59, 65, 91
opposed amphibious 49–56
persistence of x, 34, 39–56, 66, 70
political considerations 36, 45, 53–6
risks 25, 30, 48–9
simple amphibious 24, 41–5
superior ship 45–9
twentieth-century activity 40, 57, 70
& US 45–70
victims 24–5, 40
& war 25, 40, 49, 57
Haig, Alexander (1924–): US Secretary of State 37, 50

Hill, Rear Admiral Richard RN (1929–): 82, 84, 109, 136 n.4
Hitler, Adolf (1889–1945): German leader xi, 13, 15

Iceland 58, 86, 89
Imperialism xii, 7, 20, 32, 98, 105–6
India 32, 38, 55, 58, 104–5, 108–9
Indian Ocean
arms control 120
conflict in 10, 22
Diego Garcia 63
outside navies in 59–60, 63, 66–8, 101–2, 104, 108–9, 120
Réunion 108
Indochina (*see also* Vietnam War)
Cambodia 17, 19–20, 93
& communism 33
fighting in x, 4, 17, 19–20, 27, 36, 57, 128
Mekong 20
Vietnam 17, 20, 43, 78, 93–5
Indonesia
Borneo 20–1
British Chargé d'Affaires 42
& communism 33
confrontation with (1963–6) 20–1, 72
Djakarta 42
& Malacca Straits 86–7
navy 21, 37, 42–3, 82
President Sukarno 20–1, 53
Pulau Sambu 39, 41–3
strategy 20
& Timor 55
Indo-Pakistan War (1971) 22
International Institute for Strategic Studies 1, 3, 7, 23, 115
International law
Declaration of Paris 96
estate management 82–91
Geneva Convention on the High Seas 92–3, 97
International Court 84
law & order 39, 70, 82, 87
piracy 92–3
straits 15, 30, 85–8, 117–18, 121
unemployment 82

Iran (*see also* Gulf War)
Abadan 43
hostages 59–60
& Iraq 38, 58
navy 23–4, 58–9, 61–6, 68–9, 74
oil 43, 59, 61, 66
revolution 59
Shah of 59
& Soviet Union 34, 62, 66–8
& US 30, 34–5, 59–60, 65–9
Iraq (*see also* Gulf War) 23, 34–5, 38, 48, 58, 64, 67
Ireland 80, 83, 87–9, 97–8
Israel 11, 15, 17–18, 21–3, 34–5, 38, 45–8, 53, 57, 94, 119
Italy
arms control 114
Corfu 54
navy 28, 31, 54, 64, 66, 93, 97, 103–4, 109
& terrorists 94–5
& war x, 28, 31, 69

Japan
Admiral Yonai 112
Anglo-Japanese alliance 77
arms control 114
fishing 84, 90, 108
government 2
& Gulf oil 65
& gunboat diplomacy 54–5
Hiroshima 2
& Korea 38
Maritime Safety Agency 82, 90
merchant fleet 93, 108
Nagasaki 2
navy 3, 11, 28, 31, 104–5, 108, 110
shipbuilding 108
& war x, 3, 11, 13, 16, 31, 47
Johnson, Lyndon (1908–73): US President 20, 39, 48

Kaiser Wilhelm II (1859–1941) xi, 11, 77, 113, 122
Kennedy, J.F. (1917–63): US President 12, 53
Kissinger, Henry (1923–): US Secretary of State 1

Korea
  & Japan 38
  naval prowess 102
  North 18–19, 47–8, 58, 78, 82, 86
  ships 68, 84
  South 18, 33, 58, 82, 100–1
  war in (1950–3) x, 18–19, 27

Latin America (*see also named countries*) 37, 40, 86, 120, 128
Leach, Admiral of the Fleet Sir Henry (1923–) 25
League of Nations 54
Liberia 22, 61, 68, 87
Libya 30, 34, 72, 85, 99, 107, 119
Limited naval force *see* Gunboat diplomacy

Malaya (Malaysia) 20–1, 42, 86–7, 93
Malta 22, 43, 61
Marines
  Argentine 24
  British 24, 44, 87, 99
  US 50–1, 53
Maritime strategy
  convoy 65–6, 68
  influence of 2
  trade protection 57, 60–70
  of the US xi, 8–15, 29, 68, 76, 110, 126–7
Mediterranean Sea
  arms control in 119–21
  confrontation in 8, 10, 13–14, 40, 122–3
  gunboat diplomacy in 39, 45–8, 57, 69
  local navies 103, 105
  outside navies 104, 118–19
Merchant shipping 22, 24, 27, 35, 44, 54, 60–70, 86–8, 92–100
Middle East x, 21, 32, 43–8, 119, 128
Mines
  laying 20, 30, 35, 64, 69, 86, 99, 103
  sweeping 64–6, 104
Missiles
  ballistic 5, 8, 11, 115, 126

coastal 86
cruise 6, 115–16
Exocet 26–7, 35, 63–4
Poseidon 88, 116
Styx 22
submarine-launched 5, 8, 11, 115–16, 126
Tomahawk 115–16
Morocco 88
Mozambique 78

Named ships
  ACHILLE LAURO, Italian liner 94–5, 98, 100
  AGINCOURT, British destroyer 43
  AISNE, British destroyer 43
  ALABAMA, Confederate cruiser 97
  ALBATROS, French fishing escort 101
  ALBION, British carrier 19, 21, 44
  ALMIRANTE CERVERA, Spanish cruiser 122, 139 n.26
  AMBRONIA, Italian tanker 66
  AMERICA, US carrier 48, 78
  AMERICAN SPARTAN, US freighter 100
  AMOCO CADIZ, Liberian tanker 87
  ANDREA DORIA, Italian liner 83
  ANDROMEDA, British frigate 44, 109
  ANGLESEY, British patrol boat 83
  ANTELOPE, Britsh frigate 26
  ANTRIM, British destroyer 26
  ARDENT, British frigate 26
  ARGONAUT, British frigate 26
  ARKANSAS, US cruiser 29, 73
  ARMADA, British destroyer 43
  ARROMANCHES, French carrier 19
  ATLANTA, US submarine 88
  ATLANTIC CONVEYOR, British supply ship 27
  AYU-DAG, Soviet research vessel 85
  BALNY, French frigate 94
  BARHAM, British battleship 3
  BEAVER, British frigate 79
  BELGRANO, Argentine cruiser 26–7
  BEZZAVETNY, Soviet frigate 73

Named ships – *continued*

BOSTON, US cruiser 46

BOYKIY, Soviet destroyer 77

BRAMSDEN, British merchant ship 54

BRIDGETON, US tanker 64

BRIGHTON, British frigate 44

BRILLIANT, British frigate 26

BRITANNIA, Royal yacht 44

BROADSWORD, British frigate 26, 83

BULWARK, British carrier 19, 21

BURGOA MENDI, Spanish trawler 89

C. TURNER JOY, US destroyer 20

CABO SAN ANTONIO, Argentine tank landing ship 24

CALDAS, Colombian frigate 86

CANBERRA, British liner 27

CARL VINSON, US carrier 72

CARON, US destroyer 35, 73, 76

CENTAUR, British carrier 21

CHANDLER, US destroyer 68

CHAUMONT, French tanker 66

CHEQUERS, British destroyer 43

CHIEFTAIN, British destroyer 43

CHIVALROUS, British destroyer 43

CLEMENCEAU, French carrier 63

COLOMBIAN EAGLE, US cargo ship 93

CONQUEROR, British submarine 26

CONSTELLATION, US carrier 59, 63, 90

CORAL SEA, US carrier xi, 77

CORUNNA, British destroyer 43

COVENTRY, British destroyer 26

CROIX DE LORRAINE, French trawler 90

CUXTON, British minesweeper

DAVID R. RAY, US destroyer 63

DE GRASSE, French destroyer 79

DEDALO, Spanish carrier 74

DEVONSHIRE, British destroyer 44

DEWEY, US destroyer 78

DIAMOND PRINCESS, British merchant ship 44

DOMIAT, Egyptian frigate 19

DRUMMOND, Argentine frigate 24

DWIGHT D. EISENHOWER, US carrier 60, 79

EAGLE, British carrier 19, 22, 118

EASTERN POWER, Liberian tanker 68

ELROD, US frigate 68

EMILE BERTIN, French cruiser 19

ENTERPRISE, US carrier 22, 35

ESKIMO, British frigate 99

EURALYUS, British cruiser 43

EXETER, British destroyer 134 n.30

FALCON COUNTESS, US tanker 94

GEARING, US destroyer 92

GLAMORGAN, British destroyer 27

GLASGOW, British cruiser 43

GRANVILLE, Argentine frigate 24

GRAVELINES, British destroyer 43

GRECALE, Italian frigate 66

GUADALCANAL, US carrier 64

GUAM, US amphibious assault ship 49, 51

GULF STAR, Greek merchant ship 22

HALEHA BARU ADAL, Malaysian merchant ship 93

HAMPSHIRE, British destroyer 44

HARMATTAN, British merchant ship 22

HERCULES, Argentine destroyer 24

HERMES, British carrier xi, 22, 25, 27, 44

HOBART, Australian destroyer 46

HYDRA, British survey ship 44

HYUNDAI, No. 7, Korean freighter 68

IBRAHIM AL-AWAL, Egyptian destroyer 21

ILLUSTRIOUS, British carrier 79, 109

INDEPENDENCE, US carrier 51–2

INTREPID, British assault ship 109

INVINCIBLE, British carrier 25, 27, 118

IOWA, US battleship 18

ISLAND TRANSPORTER, Maldives freighter 68

Named ships – *continued*
IVAN KOROTEYEV, Soviet freighter 24, 64
IVAN ROGOV, Soviet amphibious warfare ship 77–8
JUPITER, British frigate 44
JUTLAND, British destroyer 43
KIEV, Soviet carrier 118
KIROV, Soviet battle cruiser 125
KITTY HAWK, US carrier 59
KÖNIGSBERG, German cruiser 77
KRASNY KAVKAZ, Soviet ASW ship 79
LAFAYETTE, French carrier 19
LEAHY, US destroyer 77
LENINGRAD, Soviet carrier 73–4, 76, 118
LIBERTY, US spy ship 39, 45, 52, 57
LONG BEACH, US cruiser 76
MCCANDLESS, US frigate 77
MADDOX, US destroyer 20, 47–8
MANHATTAN, US tanker 84
MANXMAN, British fast minelayer 43
MARIANNA, Greek tanker 94
MARSHAL CHUIKOV, Soviet tanker 64
MAURITIUS, British cruiser 43
MIDWAY, US carrier xi, 14, 59, 72
MINSK, Soviet carrier 77–8, 118
MISSISSIPPI, US cruiser 79
MISSOURI, US battleship 18, 63
MOELDERS, German destroyer 104
MOINESTER, US frigate 76
MONTE RUBY, Panamanian freighter 94
MORECAMBE BAY, British frigate 42
MOSKVA, Soviet carrier 118
NATHANAEL GREENE, US submarine 88
NEWCASTLE, British destroyer 44
NEWFOUNDLAND, British cruiser 19
NEW JERSEY, US battleship 18, 20, 76
NIEDERSACHSEN, German frigate 104

NIMITZ, US carrier 63
NORMAN ATLANTIC, Singapore tanker 66
NOTTINGHAM, British destroyer 109
OCEAN, British carrier 19, 43
OCHAKOV, Soviet ASW ship 79
ONSLAUGHT, British submarine 44
ORDJONIKIDZE, Soviet cruiser 78
OVERIJSSEL, Dutch destroyer 83
POLAR SEA, US icebreaker 85
PUEBLO, US spy ship 47–8, 86
PYOTR YEMTSOV, Soviet merchant ship 62
RANGER, US carrier 60
RESOLUTION, British battleship 122, 139 n.26
RHYL, British frigate 44
SAHAND, Iranian frigate 69
SAINTES, British destroyer 43
SAMUEL B. ROBERTS, US frigate 69
SANTA MARIA, Portuguese liner 92–3
SANTISIMA TRINIDAD, Argentine destroyer 24
SARATOGA, US carrier 48, 94, 100
SCOTT, US destroyer 79
SCYLLA, British frigate 68, 83, 89
SEALIFT ARCTIC, US tanker 100
SHACKLETON, British research ship 48
SHEFFIELD, British destroyer 26
SOOBRAZITELNY, Soviet destroyer 80
SOUTHERN RAIDER, Panamanian trawler 101
STARK, US frigate 35, 48, 63–4
STOCKHOLM, Swedish liner 83
SUEHIRO MARU, Japanese merchant ship 93
SVERDLOV, Soviet cruiser 78
TATNALL, US destroyer 77
TEXACO CARIBBEAN, US tanker 64
THESEUS, British carrier 19
THORN, US destroyer 76
TORREY CANYON, Liberian tanker 87
TRIUMPH, British carrier 18
UDALOY, Soviet destroyer 74

Named ships – *continued*
    VALIANT, British battleship 3
    VALLE DE ACHONDO, Spanish
        trawler 89
    VALLEY FORGE, US carrier 18
    VEINTICINCO DE MAYO, Argentine
        carrier 26–7
    VENUS CHALLENGER, Liberian
        tanker 22
    VICTORIOUS, British carrier 21–2,
        72
    VICTORY, British battleship xi
    VIDAL, British survey ship 84
    VIGO, British destroyer 43
    VIKRANT, Indian carrier 22
    VILLE D'ANVERS, French freighter
        64
    VINCENNES, US cruiser 76
    VULCANUS II, Dutch chemical
        waste ship 89
    WARSPITE, British battleship 3
    WILLIAM V. PRATT, US destroyer
        78
    WISCONSIN, US battleship 18
    WORLD PROGRESS, Liberian tanker
        68
    WORLD SPRING, Panamanian
        tanker 68
    YORK, British destroyer 68
    YORKTOWN, US cruiser 35, 73, 76
    ZHGUCHIY, Soviet destroyer 77
Nation states
    character of x, 4, 12, 32, 108
    sovereignty 54–5, 84–6
NATO
    area 65, 102
    Central Front 5–7, 9, 14, 110
    conventional defence 7
    European members 7, 88, 94, 108
    exercises 50, 75
    & Lord Carrington 128
    navies 18, 108–10
    northern flank 7, 110
    & Persian Gulf 59, 64–5
    political warning time 11, 110
    reinforcement 7, 9, 14
    southern flank 7
    Standing Naval Force Atlantic
        105
    strategy of 9, 79, 127–8
Naval Forces 104, 121, 127
Navies (*see also* British, French, *etc*)
    amphibious 10, 18, 102, 124
    ancillary 20, 36, 39
    Der Tag 101
    & distant combat 25, 29, 103,
        105–11
    exercises 12, 15, 50, 73–6, 104,
        109–10, 122–5
    flexibility of 12
    functions xii, 30–1, 44, 82, 102
    future of 30–1, 39, 91, 111, 128
    & imperialism 30, 105–6
    instruments of power 112
    less arrogant 71
    & limited war 16–31
    modern x
    negligence of 98
    neutral 22, 70
    number of x, 39, 83
    ocean-going x, 82, 102–12
    optional 21–4, 39
    & piracy x, 93–4
Nepal (& Gurkhas) 32, 42
Netherlands
    & Indonesia 20
    navy xi, 64, 92, 104–5, 108–9
    shipping 61
    & war 71
Neutrality (neutrals) 17, 22–3, 46–
    7, 61, 68, 70, 75–6, 80, 97
New Zealand 18, 21, 88
Nicaragua 36
Nicolson, Sir Arthur, later Lord
    Carnock (1894–1928): 11
Nicolson, Sir Harold (1886–1968):
    British writer 2, 130 n.21
Nigeria 44
Nixon, Richard (1913–   ): US
    President 4, 20
North Sea 12, 89, 99–100
Norway 11, 71, 75, 85, 94
Norwegian Sea 10, 124–5
Nuclear
    annihilation 1
    catastrophe 7
    depth-bombs 9
    parity 9, 14

Nuclear – *continued*
  strategy 6
  war x, 1–15
  warheads 5, 8
  weapons x, 2–15, 16, 19, 115–17,
    120, 123, 126
  winter 1

O'Connell, Professor D.P. (1924–
  79) 84, 92, 135 n.1
Orwell, George (1903–50): British
  writer 121

Pacific ocean
  navies in 104–5, 108–10
  South 89, 120
  war in 25, 105, 110
  Western 10
Pakistan (*see also* Indo-Pakistan War)
  22, 34, 38, 58, 78
Panama 94, 101
Pearson, Anthony (1941–): British
  writer 46–7, 132 n.2
Persian Gulf *see* Gulf states, war
Philippines 33, 93, 98, 119
Piracy (pirates)
  coastal waters 87
  & Gulf War 97
  hostages 93–4
  hostes humani generis 92, 95
  ideology 96
  & insurgency 92
  & naval powers x, 93–4, 96, 98,
    100–1
  political motives 92–100
  & privateers 96
  & submarines 97
  & terrorism 98–101
  Thai pirates 93, 98–9
  Vietnamese victims 93, 98
  & war 92
Poland 13, 84
Pollution 30, 84, 86–9
Portugal 32, 35, 86, 92–3, 119
Pulau Sambu (1952) 39, 41–3, 49

Queen Victoria (1837–1901) xi, 122

Reagan, Ronald (1911–): US
  President 1, 3–4, 15, 26, 35,
    39, 45, 50, 53, 57, 79, 91, 95,
    107
Romania 124
Royal Navy *see* British Navy
Rules of engagement 10, 16, 123
Russia (*see also* Soviet Union)
  Baltic Fleet 77
  Crimea 35, 73, 117
  Okhotsk 76
  Port Arthur 11, 15
  Second Pacific Squadron 3, 47
  in war 11–12
Rutherford, Lord (1871–1937):
  British scientist 2

Sailors
  ashore 28, 69
  consolation of 69
  courtesy among 54, 122–3
  Gulf casualties 23, 61
Salvador, El 53, 78
Saudi Arabia 23, 67
Second World War
  antecedents xi, 13, 97, 116
  character of 16
  Dresden 2
  invasion of Russia 11, 13
  in Pacific 25, 105
  resistance movements 98
  Tokyo 2
Showing the flag
  anniversaries 79
  better impression 80
  & diplomacy 72
  early history 71
  eyes of beholder 76
  friendly 72, 76–81, 109
  & gunboat diplomacy 71–2, 74,
    80–1, 111
  & naval recruiting x, 72
  opposition to 102
  Pepys on 71
  smartness 77
  tact 79
  unfriendly 72–6
  visits 76–81

Singapore   21–2, 39, 41–3, 66, 94, 100
Soldiers
  airborne   51
  commandos   19, 21, 44
  ideas of   13, 15, 110
  mercenary   32
  not (*repeat* not)   39, 42
  SAS   41–2
Somalia   35, 67
South Africa   29, 36
South East Asia   20–1, 42, 93–4, 120
Soviet Navy (*see also* Russia)
  admirals   6, 12, 16, 29, 77, 80, 107, 120, 124, 127
  aircraft carriers   73–4, 76–8, 117–18
  Baltic Fleet   118
  Black Sea Fleet   118
  Cam Ranh Bay   93, 119
  exercises   12, 73–5, 123–5
  expansion   8, 106
  Fifth Eskadra   35, 40
  in Gulf   58, 60, 62–6
  & gunboat diplomacy   35, 44–5, 62, 87
  Kola base   11, 115
  Mediterranean Squadron   8, 13, 22, 35, 118–19
  Northern Fleet   118, 124
  ocean-going   102, 104–7
  Pacific Fleet   78, 93
  Petropavlovsk base   115
  strategy   8, 10, 12
  submarines   8–11, 14, 48, 73, 85, 118
  tasks   8, 82–3, 102
  visits   77–80
  Vladivostok base   73, 115
  & war   xi, 8–15, 28–31
Soviet Union (*see also* Russia, Soviet Navy)
  arms control   1, 3–4, 7, 15, 115–28
  clients   34–7, 67, 92, 97, 127
  & Cuba   32–5, 74, 76
  disclosures   1
  fishing   89
  isolation   54

Kamchatka   29, 73
& Korea   18
Maritime Border Guards   82–3
merchant ships   35, 62, 64–6, 94
Montreux Convention of 1936   117–18
Moscow   4, 37
nuclear weapons   3, 5–11, 16, 115–16, 120
Ogarkov, Marshal   4
Persian Gulf   58–70
Ponomarev, Boris   7
Pravda   12, 75
President Gromyko   107, 120
Second World War   11, 13
Sokolovskiy, Marshal   8
strategy   4–15, 16
territorial waters   72–3, 83, 85, 88
& US   1, 5–15, 20, 29–30, 35, 53, 58, 60, 62, 64–8, 72–7, 85, 118–28
Vladivostok   14, 73
Spain
  Armada   xi, 30
  Basques   98
  Civil War   30, 44, 54, 69–70, 97, 122
  coastal defence   88
  fishing   84, 86, 89
  & Gibraltar   38, 74, 88
  navy   28, 30–31, 74, 122
  Nyon Agreement   97
  & US   45, 69, 105, 119
Stalin, Josef (1879–1953): Soviet leader   1, 33
Strategy (*see also* Maritime)
  & arms control   125–8
  attrition   5, 127
  'massive retaliation'   5, 7
  nuclear   3, 6, 126
  perversion of word   126
  of Super Powers   5–15, 50, 126–8
  tactics   11
  trip-wire   5
  unforeseen   110–11
  weapons   5
  withholding   8
Submarines
  aground   48, 88, 136 n.24

Submarines – *continued*
anti-submarine warfare (ASW)
8–11, 74, 97
attack 14, 26
detection of 5, 115
nuclear-powered 8
& piracy 97
in Scandinavian waters 48, 73, 85
strategic 4–6, 8, 30, 75, 110, 128
survivability of 5
Suez adventure of 1956 19, 21–2,
25
Super Powers (*see also* Soviet Union,
United States)
armed truce xii, 58
bellicose talk of 15–16
capability of 103–7
& coastal states 87
confrontation 5, 8, 10–15, 22, 35,
48, 118–23
economic strain in 106–7
flag showing 74–80
& limited war 28–30
& pirates 98
& proxy war 33–7
strategy of 6–15, 76, 126–8
victims 45
Surprise 5–8, 11, 13, 15, 53, 99
Sweden
exports arms 35, 61
navy 30, 82
& Soviet submarines 48, 73, 85
Stockholm Conference 123–4
& war 30
Syria 13, 21, 32, 35, 94

Terrorism (terrorists)
endemic 128
hostages 94
Irish 87, 89
Palestine Liberation Front 94
Palestine Liberation
Organisation 94–5, 98
& piracy x, 87, 98–101
Tamils 98
& US Navy 100–1
Thailand 93, 98
Thatcher, Margaret (1925–):
British Prime Minister 53

Third World xii, 33, 75, 106
Till, Geoffrey, British writer 82,
130 n.17, 135 n.3
Times, The x, 23, 66
Time of change ix, 56
Tirpitz, Admiral Alfred von (1849–
1930) xi, 77, 112
Turkey
& Cyprus 44, 55
& Greece 38, 58, 89, 91, 105
& Gulf War 23
Montreux Convention of 1936
117–18
Straits 117–18
& US 119

United Nations
Convention of 1982 on Law of the
Sea 91–2, 97–8
Disarmament Commission 123
Falklands War 25, 37
General Assembly 4, 120
Grenada 53
Korea 18
& national sovereignty 55
naval force 62, 105
peacekeeping forces 102
Secretary General 120
Security Council 18, 37, 53, 55,
68, 108
Study on the Naval Arms Race 75,
112, 116, 120–1, 124
United States (*see also* US Navy)
& allies 25–6, 34, 37, 53, 64, 88,
92, 110, 115, 119, 127
American Civil War 96–7
army 55
bases 93, 119
& Canada 84–5, 90
Coast Guard 82–5, 93
Delta Force 56, 95
Department of Defense 1, 12,
47–8, 59
disclosures 1
Dulles, J.F. 33
& France 36, 79
& Grenada 39, 49–53, 55–6
& Indochina 17, 20, 36, 48
& Iran 30, 59–60

United States – *continued*
  & Israel 34, 45–8, 53, 119
  & Korea 18–19, 100–1
  & Libya 30, 34, 72, 85, 107, 119
  maritime nation 57, 91, 94, 102,
    121
  & Middle East 34, 118–19
  nuclear weapons 3–11, 19, 115–
    17
  & oil 30
  Rusk, Dean 33
  Schlesinger, James 6
  & Soviet Union 1, 5–15, 20, 29–
    30, 35, 53, 58–60, 62, 64–8,
    72–7, 85, 118–28
  & Spain 45, 69, 105, 119
  strategy 4–15, 50
  & terrorists 94–5, 98, 100–1
  Truman, President 19
*United States Naval Institute
    Proceedings* 46, 64
US Navy (*see also* Named ships)
  admirals 14, 45–7, 50–1, 68, 107,
    112, 120, 125
  arms control 114–28
  Atlantic Command 75, 92
  battleships xi, 18, 63, 76
  carriers 8, 13–14, 22, 34, 59–60,
    68, 78, 94, 125
  coat-trailing 14, 50, 72–3
  deployment 10–15, 22, 63, 67–8,
    88
  & Dominican Republic 44, 55
  exercises 12, 50, 73, 75–6, 110
  expansion 57, 105–6
  gunboat diplomacy 30, 35, 39,
    45–56, 57–70, 85, 90
  Middle East Force 59, 68
  mines 20, 35, 103
  ocean going 102–7, 121
  Pearl Harbor 11, 15
  Philippine base 93, 119
  probes Russian coasts 14, 29, 35,
    85, 115, 118
  role of xi, 28, 31, 110
  Seventh Fleet 18, 20, 43, 93
  Sixth Fleet 8, 13, 22, 35, 40, 43,
    72, 85, 107, 118–19
  & Soviet Union 8–15, 22, 29–30,
    35, 67–8, 72–3, 75–7, 93, 106–
    7, 114–28
  Special Warfare Group 100
  strategy 5, 8–15, 29, 68, 76, 110,
    126–7
  task forces 8, 22
  Vietnam War 20, 35, 45, 68
USSR *see* Soviet Union

Venezuela 37, 86
Vietnam War (*see also* Indochina)
    1946–75
  casualties 17
  character of 17, 36, 58, 68, 109
  Gulf of Tonkin 20, 46–8
  Haiphong 19–20, 35
  Saigon 20, 45
Violent peace
  definition ix, xii
  era of x, 17, 22, 31, 53, 68, 83,
    107, 111, 127–8

War (*see also* First World, Vietnam,
    etc.)
  of aggression 7, 17
  barbarity 20
  casualties ix, 2, 6, 16–17, 20
  conventional 6–7, 128
  definition 16–17
  escalation 4–6, 9–10, 14, 17, 24–
    5, 30
  in Europe 5–7, 110
  global 9, 110, 126
  incidence of ix, 17–18, 30
  limited x, 5–6, 16–31, 39, 111,
    128
  local 16, 29–30
  nature of 6–7, 16–17, 23, 30
  naval x–xi, 9, 16, 18, 24–38, 39,
    111
  nuclear x, 1–16, 110, 126
  proxy x, 32–8, 39
  terminal 39
  total x, xii, 1–15, 17, 39, 68, 70,
    126, 128
  useless 15
  victory in x, 4, 9–10, 14–15, 17–
    18, 21
  war-fighting 6

Warsaw Pact 6–7, 12
Warships (*see also* Named ships)
   & arms control 112–28
   future need for 28, 86
   humanitarian tasks 44, 54, 69–70,
     83, 93–4, 102
   longevity xi, 3
   nuclear-powered 29, 63, 79, 88
   & nuclear weapons 6, 8–11, 88
   & pirates x, 95
   provoke trouble 112
   spy ships 39, 45–8, 60
Watkins, Admiral James D. USN
   (1927–): former Chief of

Naval Operations ix, 9–12, 14,
   29, 68, 102, 120–1, 129 n.1
Weinberger, Caspar (1917–): US
   Secretary of Defense xii,
   129 n.9
Woodward, Vice-Admiral Sir John
   (1932–) xi, 26

Yemen 44, 77–8
Yugoslavia 11, 77, 82, 94–5

Zimbabwe 34